BORE NO MORE!

By Mike & Amy Nappa

Vital MINISTRY™
Loveland, Colorado

DEDICATION

For our parents, Zahea Nappa and Norm and Winnie Wakefield,
who taught us that learning about God should never be boring.

CREDITS
Editor: Stephen Parolini
Senior Editor: Paul Woods
Creative Products Director: Joani Schultz
Copy Editor: Pam Shoup
Art Director: Helen H. Lannis
Cover Art Director: Liz Howe
Cover Designer: Diana Walters
Computer Graphic Artist: Randy Kady
Cover Photography: © Robert Cerri, The Stock Market
Illustrators: Vicki Logan, Bill Fisher, Randy Kady
Cartoonists: John McPherson, Rob Portlock, Randy Glasbergen, and James Cook
Production Manager: Gingar Kunkel

Library of Congress Cataloging-in-Publication Data
Nappa, Mike, 1963–
  Bore no more! : 70 creative ways to involve your audience in unforgettable Bible teaching : for every pastor, teacher, speaker / by Mike and Amy Nappa.
     p.   cm.
  Includes bibliographical references and indexes.
  ISBN 1-55945-266-8
  1. Homiletical illustrations.   I. Nappa, Amy 1963–
II. Title.
BV4225.2.N36 1995
252' .08--dc20   94-24039
                                    CIP

10 9 8 7 6 5 4   03 02 01 00 99 98 97
Printed in the United States of America.

Contents

Introduction

"My young son asked what was the highest number I had ever counted to. I didn't know but asked about <u>his</u> highest number. It was '5372.'
'Oh,' I said. 'Why did you stop there?'
'Church was over.'"
—Joanne Weil

The Visitor

● ● ● ● ● ● ● ● ● ● ● ● ● ● ● ● ● ●

THE SIGN ON THE DOOR SAID: AL LEGORY, PASTOR.

It was dark throughout the rest of the church, but the light in the pastor's office burned brightly into the night. Behind the desk, Pastor Legory flipped open books, turned pages, and recorded notes on a yellow legal pad.

Suddenly, a figure appeared in the door frame. Tall and thin, he wore an English-style overcoat and a hat that looked as if it had come straight from the haberdashery on Baker Street. He stood motionless in the doorway, puffed silently on a pipe, and waited.

Finally, Pastor Legory looked up and smiled. "Well, well! A pastor is always happy to see congregation members, but I'm surprised to see you here at this late hour."

"Watson said you had a problem. I thought maybe I could lend a hand."

Pastor Legory put down his pencil and leaned back in his chair. "Yes," he said, "maybe you can help."

"TELL ME THE FACTS," SAID THE OVERCOATED MAN.

Pastor Al opened one of the books piled on his desk. "Read this," he said.

The tall man started reading. "We polled adult church attendees to learn their perceptions of the sermon time. Here's some of what we discovered:

● 87 percent say their minds wander during sermons.

● 35 percent say the sermons they hear are too long.

● Just 12 percent say they usually remember the message."[1]

Pastor Al reached for the book. "And that's not all," he said. "Listen to this: 'People forget 40 percent of a speaker's message within 20 minutes. They forget 60 percent after a half day. And after a week they lose 90 percent.' I'm trying to teach my people about what it means to have a vibrant, active faith in God, but they're only remembering one-tenth of what I teach them. I don't know, but I'd like to think my sermons could have more impact than that."[2]

The man paused to remove his hat and set down his pipe. "You know, pastor," he said, "research indicates people retain only about 10 percent of what they learn through spoken or written communication, but they remember up to 90 percent of what they learn through direct experience.[3] Maybe it's time for you to take advantage of that information and vary the methods you use during sermon time."

"What do you mean?"

"Well, according to a recent Group Publishing poll, roughly 85 percent of adults who attend church would like to see their pastors 'try some new methods other than lecture during the sermon time.' "[4]

"That *sounds* nice. But you've been here on a Sunday morning. If I tried anything even a little out of the ordinary, my people would revolt!"

The thin man shook his head as he finally took a seat. "Actually," he said, "I'm not sure you're giving us congregation members the credit we deserve. That same poll asked people how they'd respond if their pastors used one or more new methods such as guided active-learning experiences, short dramas, object lessons, or interactive discussion during a sermon time. Nearly 90 percent said they'd be supportive and participative. That means nine of 10 people here on a Sunday morning would welcome the idea of you incorporating new methods in your sermon time."[5]

"BUT HOW DO I INCORPORATE NEW METHODS IN A SERMON?"
asked the good pastor.

From somewhere inside his overcoat, the visitor produced a worn manila envelope. Inside it was a book.

"*Bore No More! 70 Creative Ways to Involve Your Audience in Unforgettable Bible Teaching.* What's this?" asked Pastor Al.

"It's the answer to your question," replied the visitor in the overcoat. "In this book you'll find scores of active, innovative ideas to help you teach God's Word during a sermon. Interactive discussions, guided active-learning experiences, affirmation activities, object lessons, creative prayers, skits and creative readings, creative uses of music, and celebration activities. These are the things adults said they'd most like to see in a sermon, and now they're yours for the taking."[6]

"Interesting. But when do I use them?"

"The ideas in this book run about five to 10 minutes, so you can use them anytime—whenever they work best to illustrate a point you're making. For example, instead of using a story to start off a sermon, why not begin with an active-learning experience? Or you could use an object lesson to spice up the middle of a sermon. You might even try a closing affirmation or celebration activity to wrap up a sermon."

"So these ideas aren't meant to replace a sermon, but to help illustrate it?"

"Exactly," said the visitor. "And the sermon ideas are divided into four sections: ideas to help people grow in their knowledge of God, ideas to encourage positive Christian relationships, ideas that deal with Christian concerns, and ideas for special occasions. Each idea also has a 'risk rating' to help you determine what level of risk your congregation members will experience during the activity."

"Hey, that's not all," exclaimed Pastor Legory. "Look at this! Sprinkled throughout this book are notes and quotes to pastors from adults who regularly attend church—what people like best or least in sermons, why people would like their pastors to try methods other than lecture, and suggestions for improvement in sermons. Why, there are even encouraging words for pastors from people in typical American congregations."

The overcoated man smiled as he reached for his hat and pipe. "Well, it's late, and you've got a sermon to prepare. I guess I'd better be going."

"Mm-hmm," replied the pastor. He was already reading intently. "Why, I could use this idea right away—in this Sunday's sermon in fact."

The man in the overcoat stood, placed his Baker Street hat perfectly atop his head, and stepped toward the door. He paused when the pastor spoke once more.

"Wait," called Pastor Al as he momentarily put down the book. "*Bore No More! 70 Creative Ways to Involve Your Audience in Unforgettable Bible Teaching* will do more than just enhance my preaching. It'll help me bring the New Testament to life for the people in my care. Thanks."

"My pleasure," replied the visitor. Then, with a nod of his head, he was gone.

"Hmm," said the good pastor. "I could've sworn he'd say 'Elementary, my dear pastor' at least once before he left." Pastor Al shrugged. "Oh well," he said as he turned his attention back to the new book on his desk. "Now, let's see. Sunday's sermon text is Hebrews 11:1-16. Where was that idea? Aaahh, here it is on page 100, 'Get Off My Pew!' Yes, I think that'll work perfectly..."

Sources:

[1] Thom and Joani Schultz, *Why Nobody Learns Much of Anything at Church: And How to Fix It,* (Loveland, CO: Group Publishing, Inc., 1993), 189.

[2] Ibid., p. 190.

[3] Thom and Joani Schultz, *Do It! Active Learning in Youth Ministry,* (Loveland, CO: Group Publishing, Inc., 1993), 28.

[4] *A Confidential Survey of New Sermon Ideas,* a previously unpublished Group Publishing, Inc. poll of adults who regularly attend church.

[5] Ibid.

[6] Ibid.

Helpful Hints for Using This Book

Long before the fictional Sherlock Holmes came on the scene in search of clues that would reveal the truth, the Apostle Paul was bringing the truth of God to light in his writings. In his letter to the Romans, Paul shared this simple, yet profound truth:

"How, then, can they call on the one they have not believed in? And how can they believe in the one of whom they have not heard? And how can they hear without someone preaching to them?" (Romans 10:14).

For years we've been faithful in *preaching* to people about the Lord. But we've sometimes failed to preach about God in ways that maximize the potential for people to *hear* about God—ways that help them to remember, understand, and apply God's truth. With *Bore No More! 70 Creative Ways to Involve Your Audience in Unforgettable Bible Teaching,* you've got a revolutionary new tool to do just that. The ideas in this book will enable people to *hear* even more of your message, and believe in the God who inspires your sermons. Here are a few hints to help you use the ideas in this book to create meaningful sermons that people will remember for a lifetime:

1. Keep in mind that the ideas in this book aren't intended to *replace* your sermon, but to *illustrate* it. Just as you might share a story, a poem, or a few jokes during a sermon to bring home a point, you can easily substitute one of these interactive sermon illustrations to make the same point. Simply choose an idea that's focused on your chosen sermon text or topic and you're on your way. Using the activities and illustrations in this book will help your congregation remember the main point or apply the point of a sermon to their lives right away.

2. Don't expect too much too soon from your congregation. Active and interactive participation during a sermon time is a new concept for most people, so choose your illustrations wisely. You know your congregation. Don't be afraid to try something different, but don't force an idea that's obviously out of character for your people. There are 70 ideas in this book to choose from—so choose the best ones for your people.

To help you in your choices, the ideas in this book have all been ranked according to "risk level" for the congregation members. You might want to use a low-risk illustration to start. As your people become more comfortable with the interaction involved, you can progress to a medium-risk illustration, then to a high-risk activity.

3. Prepare the people in your congregation by telling them what to expect. Most people are conditioned to be passive observers during a sermon. They'll need some kind of warning to let them know it's all right to become active participants in the learning experience.

You might want to start off your sermon by saying something like, "This morning we'll be doing things a bit differently. Rather than simply talk at you, I'm going to give you an opportunity to become a part of today's sermon. You might find yourself doing something surprising, like switching seats or talking to your neighbor. But stick with me—you'll not only enjoy yourself, you just might learn something new as well!"

4. Read the entire illustration before using it. Some ideas require a few simple supplies or some preparation. You may also need to adjust an activity to fit the needs of your congregation, your building, or your sermon. For example, if you generally have large crowds or meet in a large sanctuary, you may occasionally need to make a portable microphone available for people to share ideas with the entire congregation.

5. Encourage everyone to be involved in the activities. When using small-group activities, do your best to make sure all people attending are included in a group. At times that'll mean some groups will have more than the recommended number of participants—that's OK. The suggested number of group members is just that—a suggestion. Ask congregation members to look around them and make sure everyone is in a group, visitors included. You may also want to suggest that people introduce themselves within the groups. Give family members who are attending your church service together the option of staying together in a group, or joining groups with non-family members.

6. Be careful not to embarrass anyone or put a congregation member "on the spot." The illustrations are designed to involve the listeners—not to embarrass them. Most people will follow your lead easily during a sermon illustration time. However, give people the freedom to opt out of an activity if they're not comfortable with it. Generally speaking, these people will be more likely to join in future activities once they've seen that you will safeguard their dignity.

On rare occasions, the movement required in some of the ideas may be difficult for people with physical challenges or disabilities. Be sensitive to these people's needs. Encourage other congregation members to assist those who may want and need help so everyone can benefit from the experience.

7. Feel free to adapt these ideas to a variety of settings. Although the ideas in this book are written with the typical Sunday morning sermon time in mind, they can easily be adapted for use in just about any ministry context. You can use this book to prepare for talks in Sunday school, midweek meetings, Bible studies, retreats, camps, workshops, conventions, seminars, or any other time you're scheduled to speak.

For example, if you wanted to use the "Alive and Well" idea (p. 14) in a home Bible study, you would simply poll the Bible study group members instead of polling the entire congregation. Or, if you think "Been There, Done That" on page 15 would work well in your Sunday school class, you might adapt the idea by choosing only five or six of the statements that relate to issues people in your class are dealing with currently.

The ideas in this book are meant to be used—we're not picky about where! So go ahead and use them wherever you think they'll best meet the needs of the people in your care.

8. Rely on the Holy Spirit to bring fruit out of your efforts. Remember, you aren't alone there behind the pulpit. Rely on God to help you facilitate the interactive learning experience and to bring about lasting change in the lives of your listeners.

Thanks for your commitment to God's people and willingness to be the "someone" to tell about the Lord. Now you're ready to turn the page and begin the adventure of *Bore No More! 70 Creative Ways to Involve Your Audience in Unforgettable Bible Teaching.* Enjoy!

Sermon Ideas About

Knowing God

Alive and Well

TOPIC: GOD'S WORD IS ALIVE
SCRIPTURE: HEBREWS 4:1-13

This idea will debunk the myth that God's Word is a dusty, out-of-date book that has nothing to do with people today.

A week before you plan to use this idea, take a few moments during a worship service to distribute 3×5 cards to congregation members. Ask the worship attendees to briefly describe a problem each is currently facing. For example, card holders might write things like "Facing financial difficulties due to a layoff at work" or "I'm struggling with thoughts of suicide." For privacy, instruct people *not* to put their names on their cards.

After everyone has had an opportunity to write a problem, have ushers collect the cards.

During the week, select up to 10 of these cards to be used in your sermon. Choose a variety of problems, including some from younger members of your congregation ("I'm having trouble making friends at school"), popular adult topics ("We're having discipline problems at home"), and more difficult topics ("My friend is a homosexual and I don't know what to think about it").

After you've chosen the problems, find one or more Scripture references that apply to each situation. If the topic is not directly addressed in the Bible, select a reference you believe gives guidance to the situation. List your chosen Scripture verses on separate 3×5 cards. Make enough Scripture-verse cards so each row or pew in your sanctuary can have two (you'll need to make duplicate cards).

As you begin your sermon, have ushers or other assistants distribute one Scripture-reference card to a person on each end of each row. Tell the congregation that each row should form two groups (one at each end of the row) and read the passage on their card together.

When each group has read its passage, explain that you'll be reading anonymous problems shared by members of the church.

Say: **After I read a problem, think about the passage your group read together. Then discuss with your group the answers to these questions: Does our Scripture passage offer any advice for this situation? Can we apply our Scripture to the problem? If you believe your passage applies, have the person in your group**

VIEW FROM THE PEW

What I like best about sermons is . . . *"Good illustrations that are easily remembered and emphasize the point well."*

wearing the most blue stand to share your Scripture along with any insights you gained in your group discussion.

Read the first problem. Allow a few minutes for groups to discuss their Scriptures in relation to the problem. Then let those standing read aloud the Scripture they were given and tell how it applies, or what guidance it gives. Some Scriptures may apply to more than one situation. Also, you'll have more than one group reading each passage, so several people may share similar thoughts—that's OK. Different groups may add new insights to the same passage, so allow as many to share as time allows.

Continue by reading a new problem and repeating the process for as long as time allows. You may want to choose only the number of topics you'll have time to cover (so all groups can share in the allotted time). Then continue your sermon, pointing out how the guidance found in the Bible is up-to-date and relevant to the problems your people are facing today.

Been There, Done That

TOPIC: JESUS UNDERSTANDS OUR WEAKNESSES

SCRIPTURE: HEBREWS 4:14—5:10

Use this idea to demonstrate that no matter what our experiences in life have been, Jesus has been there, too.

Begin by instructing half the congregation to stand. Explain that after you read each statement, you would like congregation members to evaluate whether or not the statement is true in their lives. If the statement is true for a person who is standing, then he or she should sit down. If the statement is true for a person who is sitting, then that person should stand up. Let everyone know that it's OK to be standing while others are sitting, and vice versa. (The reason for this varied sitting and standing method is so that no one feels singled out by standing or sitting in response to a statement.)

Warn congregation members that they'll probably end up standing and sitting several times before you're finished. Then read the statements one by one, pausing after each one to allow people to stand or sit (whichever is appropriate).

Say:

● Those of you who are standing, take your seat if you were tempted to do something you knew was wrong during this past week. If you're already seated, then stand if that statement is true for you.

● Those of you who are standing, take your seat if you believe you've made a positive difference in the life of at least one person this month. If you're already seated, then stand if that statement is true for you.

● Those of you who are standing, take your seat if you've felt misunderstood sometime during the past seven days. If you're already seated, then stand if that statement is true for you.

● Those of you who are standing, take your seat if sometime in the last 24 hours you really wanted to talk to someone, but couldn't find anyone who would listen. If you're already seated, then stand if that statement is true for you.

● Those of you who are standing, take your seat if someone was happy to see you this morning. If you're already seated, then stand if that statement is true for you.

● Those of you who are standing, take your seat if you've ever had an illness that lasted more than seven days. If you're already seated, then stand if that statement is true for you.

● Those of you who are standing, take your seat if you've ever tried to help someone but your offer was refused. If you're already seated, then stand if that statement is true for you.

● Those of you who are standing, take your seat if you had a reason to celebrate sometime during the past 30 days. If you're already seated, then stand if that statement is true for you.

After the last statement, have any standing people sit down. Then ask congregation members to think about what these experiences tell us about life. Explain that the emotions we feel in all of these experiences help define us as human—we all experience pain, joy, loss, and hope. Continue with your sermon, pointing out that because Jesus lived as a human, he understands these same joys and sorrows we've experienced.

"ONCE AGAIN, I WANT TO STRESS THAT THE SERMON ILLUSTRATION I'VE JUST GIVEN IS PURELY FICTIONAL AND IS NOT BASED UPON ANYONE HERE IN THE CONGREGATION."

Building Blocks of Faith

HIGH
MEDIUM
LOW

RISK RATING

TOPIC: JESUS, THE FOUNDATION OF OUR FAITH

SCRIPTURE: 1 PETER 2:2-10

With this object lesson, you can give your congregation members a visual demonstration of the need to build their lives on the solid foundation of Jesus.

Gather children's building blocks, one for each row in your sanctuary, and one brick (or a small piece of plywood). Place the brick (or plywood) on a table where everyone can see it. Have ushers (or other assistants) give a building block to one person in each row, choosing the recipients of the blocks at random. Tell the people who receive the blocks that they're now "builders."

Ask the builders to come forward and construct a tower on top of the brick (or plywood). Tell builders to make sure all the blocks are stacked on top of the brick (or plywood). When the group has completed this project, thank them and have them return to their seats.

Say: **Our builders have done a wonderful job constructing this tower on the foundation of this brick (or plywood). As long as this foundation remains unshaken, the building is in no danger. But if the foundation is removed** (at this point, jerk the brick or plywood from under the blocks, causing the structure to fall)**, the tower can't stand.**

Leave the blocks where they fall and continue your sermon. Emphasize the point that a life built on any foundation other than Jesus is destined to fall, because its foundation will eventually fail.

Celebrate Jesus

TOPIC: THE GREATNESS OF CHRIST

SCRIPTURE: COLOSSIANS 1:15-29, focusing on verses 15-20

This activity will help people explore Christ's greatness and echo the praises of Christ found in Colossians 1:15-29.

Have congregation members form small groups, with up to five people in each group. Let everyone know that each group will need a Bible and at least one hymnal or song book.

Say: **Read Colossians 1:15-29 aloud in your group, focusing on verses 15-20. Then, together with the other people in your group, summarize this passage in one sentence.**

Allow a couple of minutes for people to complete their summaries. Then say: **Now take your hymnal or song book and look through it for two or three songs that reflect the sentiment of the passage you've just summarized. For example, you might choose songs such as "Great Is Thy Faithfulness" or "Awesome God." Look for whole songs or any part of a song that expresses these thoughts.**

Allow a few minutes for groups to find their five songs. Next have representatives from various groups stand and tell about one song their group chose, explaining how the song expresses the theme of the passage or why the group thought this song was appropriate.

Finally, have everyone join in singing a few of the songs or choruses that groups chose. Then continue your sermon, emphasizing how we can praise Christ for his greatness every day.

Note: If only one verse of a song or just the chorus applies to the theme, sing only that part. If a group singled out only a few lines of a song, consider having that group's representative read the appropriate portion aloud. You might also want to use this activity as a way to lead into a congregational song fest!

VIEW FROM THE PEW

What I like least about sermons is . . . "Lecture."

Come Home

HIGH
MEDIUM
LOW

RISK RATING

Topic: GOD'S GRACE
Scripture: LUKE 15:11-32

In Luke 15:11-32 Jesus tells the parable of the prodigal son. Use this idea to let congregation members know that the same loving and forgiving grace described in the passage is available to them as well.

You'll need one copy of the "Come Home" handout on page 20 for every five congregation members. You'll need an envelope for each congregation member. Cut apart the five slips that say "Come Home" and fold each slip in half. Place each slip into a separate envelope and seal all envelopes.

As you begin your sermon, have ushers or other assistants distribute the envelopes, giving one to each person in attendance.

Say: **These envelopes contain a message from God. Please don't open them until I tell you to.**

Then continue with your sermon, sharing the message of grace in Luke 15:11-32. People will be naturally curious about what's in their envelopes—that's OK. That building curiosity will make the message all the more powerful when they finally open their envelopes.

As you move toward the closing of your sermon, say: **We have all, like the prodigal son, strayed from God. But God's message to us is the same as it was to the son in this story. Open your envelopes to discover God's message to you.**

After all have opened their envelopes, ask the congregation to take a couple minutes of silence to reflect on what this message means to them.

Then say: **God's message to you is a simple one: My child, come home. Take your "message from God" home with you today. Tape it on your bathroom mirror, refrigerator, or another place you'll see it each day this week and be reminded to come home to God.**

Variation: You might consider closing your sermon with a hymn or praise song about God's forgiving love, such as the hymn "Softly and Tenderly," or another song of your choice.

Directions: Photocopy and cut apart this handout
for use in the "Come Home" illustration.

My Child,
Come Home.

My Child,
Come Home.

My Child,
Come Home.

My Child,
Come Home.

My Child,
Come Home.

Eternal Evidence

HIGH
MEDIUM
LOW

RISK RATING

Topic: NOTHING CAN SEPARATE US FROM GOD
Scripture: ROMANS 8:31-39

Use this idea to help your people see that nothing can separate us from the love of God.

When you are ready to make this point during your sermon, say: **I'd like everyone to find a partner and discuss evidence that God's love is with us. You might think of things you'd find outdoors or things within the walls of this building.**

If you have a smaller congregation, consider actually sending pairs outdoors or around the church to search for evidences of God's presence.

After five minutes, have volunteers share what they discussed or observed. For example, a child's smile, a flower blooming, or a letter from a missionary might have reminded people of God's presence.

Then continue your sermon, explaining that although we can't physically see God, we can see evidence of his love all around us. Therefore, we can take confidence in knowing that no matter where we are, God's love is always with us.

Variation: If your congregation is too large to have everyone leave and return within five minutes, but you want them to do more than discuss the concept, have each pew or row choose a representative to go on this search. Then sing a hymn or chorus while the representatives are out of the room. When they return, have them report first to the people in their rows, then have several share with the entire congregation.

VIEW FROM THE PEW

I'd like to see my pastor try some new methods other than lecture because . . . "Any teaching that helps me remember and apply God's Word is profitable."

21

God's Green Thumb

TOPIC: SPIRITUAL GROWTH

SCRIPTURE: MATTHEW 13:1-23

This idea, building on the parable in Matthew 13:1-23, compares growth in plants to spiritual growth in Christians.

Photocopy the "Gardening Quiz" handout (p. 23) and include it in the bulletin for the day of your sermon.

During the sermon, tell everyone you have a pop quiz for them. Then allow a couple of minutes for people to take this gardening quiz.

After people have completed the quiz, share the correct answers below with the congregation.

Answers to the questions on the "Gardening Quiz" handout are:

1. False. It just takes more work to keep the ground damp.
2. False. Damp soil is best.
3. True.
4. True.
5. False.
6. True.
7. True. It kills bacteria and even chases away some bugs.

For fun, award a trowel or bag of potting soil to the person who gets the most correct answers.

Then say: **Whether or not you're a master gardener, there's one kind of growing anyone here can do—spiritual growing. God has the greenest thumb around and can grow even the most stubborn soul. Let's find out what we can do to improve the growing conditions.**

Continue with your sermon as planned. As you move through the rest of the sermon, make references to the quiz. Several of the questions can be paralleled to spiritual growth. For example, question #2 refers to the amount of water a plant needs. You may compare drowning a new plant to dumping unreasonable expectations on a new Christian. Each plant, and each person, will grow with the right amount of care. Not too much, not too little.

GARDENING QUIZ

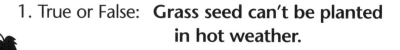

1. True or False: **Grass seed can't be planted in hot weather.**

2. True or False: **Newly planted seeds should be kept in soggy soil.**

3. True or False: **Fruits can be grown indoors.**

4. True or False: **Plants need dark as well as light.**

5. True or False: **Berry vines need different soil than other garden plants.**

6. True or False: **Plants need room to grow.**

7. True or False: **Keeping plants clean with soap and water helps them to grow.**

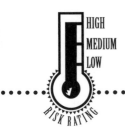

HIGH
MEDIUM
LOW
RISK RATING

Heavenly Celebration

TOPIC: PRAISING GOD

SCRIPTURE: REVELATION 5:11-14

Revelation 5:11-14 tells about heavenly creatures shouting praise to God—a scene that might be similar to the celebration after a sports victory. Use this idea to give your congregation a taste of the enthusiastic praise they can look forward to in heaven.

VIEW FROM THE PEW

One encouraging thought I'd like to share with people who deliver sermons is . . . "You probably have a lot of wisdom to share. Say it in an interesting way and I'll appreciate being challenged."

As you present your sermon on this passage, compare praising God to fans cheering after their team wins a sporting event. It can be exciting to hear fans loudly shouting their devotion and celebrating victories in the playing field. Tell your listeners that Christians have something far greater to cheer and celebrate—God! Then consider using one or more of these ideas during the sermon to create your own "heavenly celebration":

● Hand out helium balloons. Some Christian book stores carry balloons with printed slogans such as "Praise God!" or "Hallelujah!"

● Sing several energetic and upbeat worship songs, encouraging everyone to make a joyful noise to the Lord.

● Lead your congregation in a cheer to God. Have one side of the church stand, raise their hands, and yell, "Honor and glory!" Then have the other side respond by standing, raising their hands and yelling, "And praise to the Lamb!"

● Encourage members of the congregation to stand and offer short prayers of praise and thanks to God.

● Read Revelation 5:11-14 aloud, asking your congregation to join in as if they were the thousands of voices in verses 12 and 13. Encourage everyone to read loudly as the passage indicates.

● Have congregation members spend 30 seconds exchanging high fives with as many people as they can. Each time a person gives a high five, have him or her say, "Worthy is the Lamb!"

● Give God a 30-second standing ovation, complete with whistles and shouts.

I'd Know That Voice Anywhere!

HIGH
MEDIUM
LOW

RISK RATING

TOPIC: JESUS, THE GOOD SHEPHERD

SCRIPTURE: JOHN 10:1-30

Use this idea to help congregation members gain a better understanding of what it means to "hear the Shepherd's voice."

Ask for eight volunteers. Have these people come to the front of the sanctuary and state their names for everyone to hear. (You may want to write their names on a sheet of paper for your own reference.) Next, have an usher lead the volunteers outside the sanctuary into an area where they'll be unable to see or hear what's happening with the rest of the congregation.

Designate eight sections in your congregation (the sections don't have to be equal in size) and assign each section the name of one of the volunteers.

Say: **The volunteers who have left the room are "shepherds" and you are all their "sheep." When the shepherds return to the sanctuary, they'll try to get you to clap. Respond only if your assigned shepherd is addressing your section. Ignore all others.**

Have the volunteers return to the room. Point out the eight sections and say to the volunteers: **You're shepherds in search of your sheep. To find which sheep belong to you, move to the front of a section in the room, raise your hands to the people in front of you, and say, "I am (name), your shepherd. Clap for me." If the people clap, you've found your flock. If they don't respond, move on until you find your sheep.**

Have the shepherds each choose a section. When all shepherds are in place, instruct them to (one at a time) raise their hands and say their lines. See which shepherds have found their flocks (if any), then give shepherds who didn't locate their sheep 15 seconds to switch places and try again. Repeat the process until the entire congregation claps when the shepherds say their lines.

Afterward, thank the shepherds and allow them to return to their original seats. Continue your sermon, pointing out that just as congregation members responded only to their assigned shepherds, Christians ought to respond first and foremost to the voice of Christ, the Good Shepherd.

HIGH
MEDIUM
LOW

RISK RATING

I Predict...

TOPIC: GOD'S WILL FOR OUR FUTURE

SCRIPTURE: JAMES 4:14-17

VIEW FROM THE PEW

I'd like to see my pastor try some new methods other than lecture because... *"We learn more from participation."*

Use this idea to remind people that only God knows what the future will bring.

Before your sermon, gather three slips of paper and three pens. You'll also need a stopwatch or a watch with a second hand.

During the sermon, ask for three volunteers from the congregation. (For added fun, ask for volunteers who consider themselves very punctual people.) Have these three people join you up front. Give each volunteer a slip of paper and pen.

Say: **I'd like each of you to predict how long it will take for every person here to stand, shake hands with five other people, and return to their seats. Write your prediction in minutes and seconds on your paper. Keep this a secret from everyone else.**

After each volunteer has written his or her prediction, remind the congregation again of their part in this: to stand and shake hands with five others, then return to their seats.

When everyone is ready, pull out your stopwatch, give the congregation a go-ahead sign, and begin timing. Stop timing when all people have returned to their seats.

Report how much time actually passed, and have the volunteers reveal their predictions to see how close they came to guessing the correct time. Then thank the volunteers and have them return to their seats.

It's unlikely that anyone will have predicted accurately—to the second—how long the activity would take. Continue your sermon, reminding everyone that our planning and predicting will often be wrong, but God always knows what's coming. We need to trust wholeheartedly in God's ability to guide us into the future.

Let Your Fingers Do the Walking

HIGH
MEDIUM
LOW

RISK RATING

TOPIC: THE PURPOSE OF SCRIPTURE

SCRIPTURE: 2 TIMOTHY 3:14—4:5

Use this idea to demonstrate the power found in reading the Bible. To make this point you'll need two local phone books. You'll be taking pages out of one of the phone books and distributing them to congregation members to illustrate how the broad scope of the Bible is like that of a phone book.

The week before your message, look through your phone book to find what information is included in it. Some phone books list local recreation areas, tell how to turn off gas in case of emergency, give first-aid tips, or even show seating charts for local theaters and sports arenas.

From one phone book, remove enough pages so that each member of your congregation can have one. (For quick page removal, cut the binding off by running a craft knife down the bound edge—cutting through several pages at once, or have the binding cut off at a print shop.) Have the phone book pages folded and inserted in the bulletins for the appropriate week.

Note: To make this sermon idea work, plan ahead what your "story" will be and be sure pages from the phone book relating to this need are distributed. You may want to put the bulletins with these pages near the top of the pile to be sure they're taken. Also, choose topics that will have several pages of information such as restaurants or physicians so more people can participate.

On the appointed day, as you move to the front of the room to begin speaking, carry the second uncut phone book with you. Set it in an obvious place where it can be easily seen by the people in the congregation. Begin telling about the frustrations of your week. This can be a true story or an obviously fictitious one such as this:

You won't believe the troubles I've been having this week! And I don't know where to turn for help! First of all, our water heater sprung a leak and I don't know any plumbers! I waited around for a while hoping one would knock on my door, but after wading through the water for several hours, I gave up on that and tried plugging the leak with a towel. It's awful! Does anyone here know any good plumbers? If you do, just yell out their names and tell me how to reach them!

At this point, open up the conversation to the congregation, pleading for help. As soon as they catch on, those with Yellow Pages listing plumbers will begin calling out information. If you're concerned they might not catch on right away, have an informed "plant" in the congregation who'll supply the requested information from his or her phone book page at the appropriate time.

Continue your conversation, complaining about not being able to contact a friend, wondering how to bandage a wound, and so on. Again, be as diverse as your phone book allows. After several rounds of this, with congregation members providing the needed information, pick up your own copy of the phone book.

Say: **You know, I could have saved myself a lot of trouble if I'd only looked in here. I've had this book around my house all week but never bothered to open it. Of course, some of you might say the same thing about this book.**

At this point, hold up a Bible and continue with your sermon.

"GOOD MORNING. TODAY'S SERMON DEALS WITH MODERN SOCIETY'S SHORT ATTENTION SPAN. THE END. AMEN."

My Response

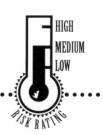
TOPIC: OUR RESPONSE TO GOD
SCRIPTURE: 2 TIMOTHY 2:8-13

In this creative reading, the congregation copies the pantomimes of several leaders. About a week before your sermon, select two or more pantomime leaders and give each leader a photocopy of the "My Response" handout on page 30. Encourage leaders to become comfortable with the motions described on the handout. Let leaders know that they won't be required to speak any words. They'll simply do the motions for the congregation to follow.

At the appropriate time during the sermon, have the pantomime leaders join you in front of the congregation. Have the leaders stand so everyone has a clear view of at least one leader. Then instruct the congregation to stand and spread out if possible.

Explain to the congregation that you will be reading from 2 Timothy and that you'd like them to respond to the words by following the actions of the leaders. Then read the bold-faced type as indicated in the "My Response" handout, pausing to allow the images of the pantomime to sink in.

Afterward, thank and dismiss the pantomime leaders and have everyone be seated. Continue with your sermon. If you like, use the motions during parts of your sermon to remind the congregation of the passage.

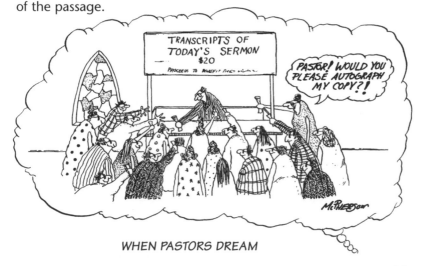

WHEN PASTORS DREAM

MY RESPONSE

 **This teaching is true: If we died with him** *(leader stands with arms outstretched, feet together, and head hanging as if on the cross),*

 we will also live with him *(lift head and look upward, reaching hands to the sky, as if reaching to heaven);*

 if we endure *(move fists to chest as if feeling pain),*

 we will also reign with him. *(Spread arms wide as if indicating a vast expanse of land.)*

 If we disown him *(cross arms and shake head in refusal),*

 he will also disown us *(motion as if slamming a door, then freeze in this position until next motion);*

 if we are faithless *(lower hands to sides and move head about looking in various directions as if distracted),*

 **he will remain faithful** *(stretch arms out to congregation with a smile and motion toward your- self as if welcoming them home),*

 **for he cannot disown himself.** *(Freeze with arms outstretched to the congregation.)*

Part of the Family

HIGH
MEDIUM
LOW

RISK RATING

TOPIC: GOD, OUR FATHER

SCRIPTURE: GALATIANS 4:4-7

Begin planning for this idea several weeks ahead. You'll need one or more animals that can be adopted by members of your congregation. Contact a local animal shelter or the office of your local Humane Society for assistance in finding animals. (Or, if your cat just had kittens . . .)

You may also wish to prepare your congregation for this event by adding a note in the church bulletin one or two weeks ahead. Without going into the details of your sermon, state that pets will be available for adoption on the appropriate date. Also include information about any fees that might be charged by the animal shelter.

During your sermon, as you're focusing on what it means to be God's child, have someone bring out the animals. Be sure animals are appropriately caged to avoid any accidents. Introduce each animal by telling its name and any other pertinent information about the pet (such as "loves children" or "needs a big backyard to run in").

Inform everyone that these animals are without homes, and unless they are adopted they will probably be killed. Point out that you're not intending to cause guilt, but merely stating a fact. Then explain the process and the costs of adopting one of the pets.

Next, ask if anyone is willing to pay the price to adopt one of these animals and take it home as a new member of the family. Wait to see if anyone responds (it's OK if no one does). If someone does indicate an interest, tell him or her where to make appropriate arrangements after the service. Let people know where the animals will be after the service in case they'd like a closer look.

Thank your helpers and have them take the animals out of the sanctuary. Then ask congregation members to tell a partner their answers to these questions:

● **What hesitations did you have about adopting a new pet today?**

● **Why do you think God is so willing to adopt us into his family on a moment's notice?**

VIEW FROM THE PEW

What makes a sermon memorable for me is . . .
"A great illustration."

Ask a few pairs to share the results of their discussions. Then continue with your sermon, using the adoption of a pet as an object lesson to picture how God adopts us into his family. Just as the new pet owner will have many responsibilities and joys, God cares for us and delights in our growth. Point out the parallels between the animals facing death and our hopeless situation without adoption by God.

If none of the animals were adopted, use this as a teachable moment and remind your congregation that God doesn't leave anyone stranded who wants to be his child—God always makes room for one more "stray."

After your service, talk to people who decided to adopt a pet. Most will be glad to have the new pet, but check to be sure they weren't feeling pressured into adopting an animal they really didn't want.

Praying Walls

TOPIC: GOD'S POWER AND LOVE

SCRIPTURE: EPHESIANS 3:14-21

Use this activity to encourage your congregation to follow Paul's example of prayer in Ephesians 3:14-21. If you use this as a closing, consider ending your sermon at least 10 minutes early to allow time for prayer.

Before your sermon, prepare four signs using the "Praying Walls" handouts on pages 33-34. To make these signs, photocopy the handouts from this book and enlarge them using an enlarging copier. Or you may make overhead transparencies (and use overhead projectors for each sign). Or you may use a wide marker to write the information in large letters on separate sheets of newsprint or poster board. Choose the option that best suits your congregation.

Before your sermon, post these signs on the four walls of your sanctuary.

During the sermon, when you're ready to begin the activity, say: **Let's follow Paul's example of prayer found in Ephesians 3:14-21, asking God to make this passage come alive for us.**

There are four signs posted around this room. Take a few moments now to quietly move to a sign, read it, and follow the prayer instructions written there.

(continued on p. 35)

PRAYING WALLS

·Sign #1

"For this reason I kneel before the Father, from whom his whole family in heaven and on earth derives its name" (Ephesians 3:14-15).

After reading the Scripture, thank God for giving you the privilege of being called his child. Tell God what being his child means to you.

·Sign #2

"I pray that out of his glorious riches he may strengthen you with power through his Spirit in your inner being, so that Christ may dwell in your hearts through faith" (Ephesians 3:16-17a).

Pray that God will strengthen you spiritually. Ask God to make his love evident in your life so all who know you will remember your loving heart and faith.

·Sign #3

"And I pray that you, being rooted and established in love, may have power, together with all the saints, to grasp how wide and long and high and deep is the love of Christ, and to know this love that surpasses knowledge—that you may be filled to the measure of all the fullness of God" (Ephesians 3:17b-19).

Try to imagine the greatness of Christ's love. Thank God for demonstrating this love to you.

·Sign #4

"Now to him who is able to do immeasurably more than all we ask or imagine, according to his power that is at work within us, to him be glory in the church and in Christ Jesus throughout all generations, for ever and ever! Amen" (Ephesians 3:20-21).

What request do you have that seems impossible? Thank God for his incredible power and ask him to go beyond your imagination in answering your prayer.

Have congregation members move to different signs every two or three minutes to be sure everyone gets the opportunity to pray at each wall. Then continue your sermon as planned. Leave the prayer signs up in case congregation members want to come by the church and spend more time in prayer during the week.

Note: If you want to use this prayer activity as a closing to your sermon, but are worried that people may leave before praying, have ushers leave the doors to the sanctuary closed. Or tell the congregation they have 10 minutes to complete the activity, then they'll need to return to their seats for a closing song or thought.

Telling the Colorful Story

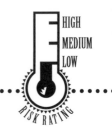

TOPIC: GOD'S MERCY

SCRIPTURE: 1 TIMOTHY 1:12-17

In the first century, the Apostle Paul vividly described God's mercy in a letter to his young friend, Timothy. In the 20th century, David Eden vividly described God's mercy in colors and music when he wrote "The Coloring Song." Use both this passage in Paul's letter to Timothy and David Eden's song to illustrate God's mercy to the people in your congregation.

If your church is unfamiliar with "The Coloring Song," have your music leader use the words and accompaniment on page 36 to teach the song to your congregation.

At the appropriate time during your sermon, say: **I'd like us to sing a song that uses color to describe the mercy Paul talks about in 1 Timothy 1:12-17. If you are wearing any color mentioned as we sing, stand and remain standing during the song when your color is mentioned.**

When the song is over, have anyone who is still seated join the others in standing. Say: **No matter what we look like, what we wear, or what we've done, God has extended mercy to us all. Think about which color from the song describes the kind of mercy you need today.** (Pause.) **Now silently pray for God to grant you that mercy. Sit down when you've finished praying.**

After everyone is seated again, continue with your sermon.

One encouraging thought I'd like to share with people who deliver sermons is . . . "Thanks for your dedication to sharing God's Word."

THE COLORING SONG

Words and Music by
David Eden

Undeserved Love

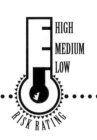

TOPIC: GOD'S LOVE

SCRIPTURE: ROMANS 5:1-19, focusing on verse 8

You'll need two sheets of blank paper per person. Half-sheets are fine. You may want to insert these in the bulletins to speed the distribution. Each person will also need a pen or pencil.

This idea focuses on the fact that God loves us even when we don't deserve it. As you make this point in your sermon, say: **Think of a person in your life who loved you when you didn't deserve to be loved.**

Give examples of such a person to clarify what you mean. For example, perhaps a neighbor cared enough to give you odd jobs for cash when you were a teenager, even though you'd accidentally broken one of her garage windows with a baseball. Or the person you married loved you enough to overlook a variety of faults and spend his or her life with you.

Allow a moment for everyone to think of a person. Then say: **Take one of the sheets of paper you were given and write a short letter to this person, thanking that person for his or her love. Write your letter even if this person is no longer living or a part of your life.**

Give up to five minutes for people to write their letters.

Say: **Now think of a time God loved you when you didn't deserve it. Write another note on the other sheet of paper, expressing your thanks for this undeserved love.**

Allow several more minutes for people to write this letter to God.

When everyone has finished, instruct congregation members to make every effort to deliver the first letters in the coming week. This may involve a bit of research, but encourage people to make the effort. If the person is no longer living, have the writer share the letter and the memory of his or her chosen person with a friend or family member.

Have people take home their second letters and tape them to bathroom mirrors, refrigerators, or other places where they'll see the letters each day this week. Encourage people to let their notes to God serve as reminders of God's love to all, no matter how much this love is not deserved. Then continue your sermon.

I'd like to see my pastor try some new methods other than lecture because . . . "There are different ways of challenging people to move closer to Jesus other than simply talking at them."

Wish List for Life

TOPIC: GOD'S PRIORITIES
SCRIPTURE: 2 PETER 3:8-13

Use this idea to help congregation members better understand that people are a high priority with God. You'll need to collect up to 10 items that either have or represent value. For example, you may want to gather things like a diamond ring, a "certificate" good for $1 million a year for the rest of your life, a drink of water from the Fountain of Youth, a coupon for a happy and fulfilling family life, a briefcase that represents a successful career of your choice, a guarantee for a satisfying relationship with God, and so on.

Before your sermon, set up a table near the pulpit with all your chosen items. Label each item with a placard that's visible to the congregation.

At the appropriate time during your sermon, have ushers distribute 3×5 cards.

Say: **You've probably heard of the Home Shopping Network, the TV channel that sells all kinds of products to its viewers. Today, I'd like us to pay a visit to the "Church Shopping Network."** (Motion to the table.) **On this table there are several of life's greatest treasures.** (Briefly describe each item.) **If you could obtain any three items on this table, which of these treasures would have the highest priorities for you? Right now, select the three items that you'd say are the most important in life and rank them in order.**

Give everyone a few minutes to make his or her choices. Then have congregation members choose a partner sitting either in front of or behind them. Have partners take turns telling which three items were their highest priorities and why.

Afterward, say: **It may be surprising to hear, but God has priorities, too. Second Peter 3:8-13 reveals that God's priority is people. God has the power and the right to destroy this world because of sin. Yet God patiently delays his judgment for one reason—so that more people can have their hearts and lives changed by the renewing power of Christ's sacrifice for sin.**

Continue your sermon, encouraging each person to take advantage of the truth that he or she is God's priority by beginning or growing in a relationship with God.

Your License Please

HIGH
MEDIUM
LOW

RISK RATING

TOPIC: GOD IS ALL-KNOWING

SCRIPTURE: 1 CORINTHIANS 2:1-11, especially verses 6-11

These verses in 1 Corinthians remind us that God knows everything. To illustrate the point that we can't keep secrets from God, form groups of up to three people.

Next, instruct each person to take out his or her driver's license. (Don't be surprised if some congregation members groan or think you're only kidding. You may have to gently encourage people more than once before they actually pull out those licenses.) Tell those people who don't drive to get out another form of identification, preferably one with a picture.

Say: **Without covering the picture or information on your ID, show it to those in your group now.** (Again, be prepared to encourage people a few times to overcome their desire to hide their pictures.)

When all have shown their pictures, ask the following questions and have people discuss their answers in their groups. You might want to write the questions on an overhead projector or on a handout to go in the bulletin for groups to refer to during discussions.

● **What secrets does your license reveal about you that you'd rather others not know?**

● **Why do we try to hide a piece of plastic that tells others what they can already see for themselves?**

After discussion, continue your sermon pointing out that many of us would like to keep secret certain facts about ourselves. But God, through the Holy Spirit, knows everything. There is nothing about ourselves that can be hidden from God's view—not even a driver's license in a wallet!

VIEW FROM THE PEW

What I like best about sermons is . . . "To feel that I have learned something new."

Sermon Ideas About
Christian Relationships

All Together?

HIGH
MEDIUM
LOW

RISK RATING

TOPIC: UNITY

SCRIPTURE: EPHESIANS 4:1-6

This activity demonstrates that no matter how diverse we are, we still have a common bond in our faith in Jesus Christ.

Start the activity by saying: **I'm going to say four words, and as I say each word I'll point to an area of the sanctuary designated for that word. Decide which word best represents your interests and move to that area.** (Point to the designated area, such as a grouping of pews or the four corners of the room, as you say the appropriate word.)

- sports
- food
- books
- music

When everyone has moved to the chosen section, say: **Now I'd like each of these groups to divide into more specific sections. Sports group, divide according to favorite sports such as football, basketball, hockey, and so on. Food group, divide according to tastes such as Chinese, Mexican, Italian, seafood, and so on. Books, divide according to genre such as mystery, biography, romance, and so on. Music, divide according to styles such as pop, rhythm and blues, symphony, and so on.**

When groups have formed accordingly, ask them to form still smaller and more specific groups such as favorite football teams, favorite fast food restaurants, favorite mystery authors, and favorite singers. (This may mean some people will be a group of one if no one else shares their interests.)

When everyone is finished, say: **Look at the vast differences we represent. We could also divide according to political differences, business differences, social views, and so on. But there is one factor we all have in common—our love for Jesus Christ. The bond we share through Jesus brings us all together into one family.**

Have everyone join hands with those around them until all groups are joined. Then sing a song of unity such as "They Will Know We Are Christians by Our Love" or "The Bond of Love." Have congregation members return to their seats as you continue with your sermon.

Church-Pew Fire Drill

TOPIC: THE BODY OF CHRIST

SCRIPTURE: 1 CORINTHIANS 12:12-27

As you are discussing the various roles each Christian plays in the body of Christ, use this activity to bring home the importance of Christians working together in service to God.

Say: **When you were young, you may have participated in a wacky "fire drill" where everyone jumped out of a car, ran around the car, and then returned to a new seat. Well, I'd like us to do a variation of that here.**

In a moment I'm going to ask members of a few rows to leave their rows, exiting from their left, and then returning to their seats from the right end of the row. This is a simple task, merely walking around your pew and returning to your seat. However, there are a few things you must consider.

If your birthday is in January, February, March, or April, you are not able to use your hands or arms in any way during this short journey.

If your birthday is in May, June, July, or August, you must close your eyes for the whole trip. Go ahead and close them now. No peeking!

And those of you who have birthdays in September, October, November, or December must walk backward all the way around the pew.

When everyone understands the guidelines, go into the congregation and choose a few rows or pews to send on the fire drill. If you have a small congregation, send all congregation members on the drill. Allow elderly members the option to pass on the activity (or participate in whatever way they choose). Caution congregation members to move quickly, but safely, being careful not to knock over anyone near them.

Then have people who participated in the fire drill spread out among the congregation to form small groups. If all congregation members participated, simply have them form small groups where they sit.

Say to those who participated in the drill: **In your group, tell about your little journey. What made the trip difficult or easy for you? Did anyone help you? Why or why not?**

*What I like best about sermons is...
"They can bring to vivid life the reality of God's Word."*

Allow a short time for discussion. If you like, have volunteers tell the entire congregation about their experiences. Then continue with your sermon, relating the activity to the message of 1 Corinthians 12:12-27. Point out that we all have different abilities which causes us to rely on each other for help. If we work together as God intended, our church, like a body, functions properly. If we aren't helping each other, everyone suffers.

GLASBERGEN

"IT'S A PROVEN FACT THAT EXERCISE MAKES PEOPLE MORE ALERT. THAT"S WHY WE DO ALL THAT KNEELING AND STANDING BEFORE MY SERMON."

Do Likewise

HIGH
MEDIUM
LOW

RISK RATING

TOPIC: WHO IS YOUR NEIGHBOR?

SCRIPTURE: LUKE 10:25-37

Jesus used the parable of the good Samaritan to answer the question, "Who is my neighbor?" Use this idea to help people identify the "neighbors" who are a part of your church.

After discussing Luke 10:25-37 in your sermon, say: **Let's take a moment right now to recognize the people who have been "neighbors" for us. If a person who has helped you grow spiritually is here today, go over and thank that person right now.**

Wait a moment for people to begin moving. Then continue:

If someone here warmly welcomed you to this church, go thank that person now. Between all the remaining statements, wait only about 30 seconds for people to move. It's not necessary to wait for people to return to their seats before giving the next instruction. You might even want to put the instructions on an overhead transparency for people to refer to during this activity. If you do, cover the items on the transparency and reveal them one by one about every 20 to 30 seconds.

Say:

If someone here brought you a meal when you were sick or in need of food, that person acted as your neighbor. Get up and thank him or her right now.

If a person here helped you move into a new home, thank him or her now for being your neighbor.

If you know someone was praying for a specific need in your life, thank that person for being your neighbor right now.

If a person here watched your kids so you could have an evening out, thank that person now for being your neighbor.

If someone here listened to you or provided a shoulder to cry on, thank that person now for being your neighbor.

Give congregation members a few seconds to finish their conversations, then ask people to return to their seats.

Say: **Now that you have recognized the people who have been "neighbors" in your life, let's hear Jesus' instruction: "Go and do what he [the neighbor] did." Be a neighbor to someone this week.**

Continue with the rest of your sermon.

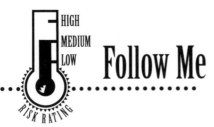

Follow Me

TOPIC: DIVISION IN THE CHURCH

SCRIPTURE: JUDE 17-25

Use this idea to help your congregation understand and apply Jude's instruction for reacting to those who cause division in the church.

As you prepare for your sermon, discuss the first point of your sermon with a respected person in your congregation. This could be your spouse, an associate pastor, or another person who is widely known. Determine how this person can disagree with your point in a convincing manner.

For example, suppose you are talking about Jude 24 and God's strength and ability to keep us from falling. Someone could refute this by saying God doesn't really help us, but we help ourselves. The person could say that we should be strong enough ourselves. Then this person could begin telling about self-help books that will teach people how to rely on themselves.

Be sure your accomplice feels comfortable with his or her task.

Early in your sermon as you make the agreed-upon point, have your accomplice stand up from his or her seat, interrupt you, and say something such as: **Excuse me. I know my speaking here is out of turn, but I just can't go on listening to this. I have to disagree with our pastor on this point and here's why.**

NOTE: You may want to let congregation members know ahead of time that someone is going to interrupt the message with a differing opinion. It's best not to trick the congregation into believing you're in the middle of an actual argument. Another way to make the activity work is to be sure your accomplice "hams it up" when arguing (so it's obvious to everyone that it's not a real argument). Or you may plan the entire activity as a skit (with you and your accomplice arguing the opposite sides of the issue).

After the accomplice explains his or her opinion, have congregation members discuss with a partner the thoughts that went through their heads during this interruption.

After discussion, continue with your sermon. Explain that while people are usually not so open with their opposition to our faith, they still cause division in other ways. Then discuss Jude's advice in Jude 17-25, pointing out ways the Bible says to deal with divisive people.

What I like least about sermons is . . . "Not being able to remember them."

It's Under the Tree!

TOPIC: SUPPORTING CHRISTIAN WORKERS

SCRIPTURE: 3 JOHN 5-8

Third John 5-8 encourages Christians to support those in service to God. Use this affirming project to give the members of your congregation an opportunity to support the ministries of your church.

A week or two before your sermon, distribute 3×5 cards to each of the volunteer workers from your congregation—Sunday school teachers, youth group leaders, social coordinators, groundskeepers, and so on. Ask these people to write their names, their volunteer responsibilities, and one needed "gift" they'd like to have to help them do their ministry.

For example, a Sunday school teacher might request the gift of a substitute one Sunday a month. A youth leader may ask for a gift of new sports equipment for youth events. The nursery coordinator might need quality children's books or even a supply of disposable diapers. Groundskeepers caring for the church property might need extra hands one morning for planting new flowers.

Ask your volunteers to return their cards to you by a designated date. Hang the cards on a real or artificial Christmas tree in the sanctuary (much like Prison Fellowship's "Project Angel Tree"). Be sure to put the tree in a visible and accessible area. You may want to place the tree beside the pulpit during your sermon so you can refer to it easily.

During your sermon, as you discuss 3 John 5-8, point out how John commended Gaius for his support of Christian workers. Then tell your congregation that they now can follow Gaius' example and support God's work in your church.

Say: **God doesn't ask only a few to serve him. He wants all of us to be involved. You may not be able to make the same commitment our volunteers have, but you can commit to supporting those active in volunteer ministry here at our church.**

Read a few of the requested "gifts" hung on the tree. Then encourage people to look over the rest of the needs on the tree after the service. Ask people to commit to meeting the need on one card by promising to provide the requested "gift" for the volunteer worker. Have people signify their commitment by removing a card from the tree. Ask people to bring their gifts and cards back to the tree within two weeks.

Two weeks later, hold a volunteer appreciation time during your worship meeting and distribute the gifts (including "certificates" good for a gift of service) to the appropriate people. Allow those receiving the gifts a few moments to thank the congregation for following Gaius' example in 3 John 5-8.

Just Do It!

HIGH
MEDIUM
LOW

RISK RATING

TOPIC: **SHOWING LOVE**

SCRIPTURE: **1 JOHN 4:7-12**

This passage directs Christians to show love toward one another. Use this activity to help people show love in a simple and immediate way.

Have everyone form groups of no more than four. Give each group two to three minutes to brainstorm ways their groups could show love to others in the congregation right then and there. For example, they could pray for someone, quickly go outside and wash a few car windows, give a group hug, share a Scripture, and so on.

When time has passed say: **Now you have five minutes to choose one of these ideas and do it! Be back in your seats five minutes from now. Go!**

Encourage groups to go immediately and act on one of their ideas. Have praise songs playing in the background while people put their thoughts into action. Afterward, continue your sermon, explaining how what they just did was an example of what John described in 1 John 4:7-12. Encourage congregation members to make showing love to others a natural response to God's love for them.

VIEW FROM THE PEW

One encouraging thought I'd like to share with people who deliver sermons is . . . "Be willing to risk (change)—we'll still love you!"

May I Be of Service?

HIGH
MEDIUM
LOW

RISK RATING

TOPIC: **SERVING OTHERS**

SCRIPTURE: **JOHN 13:1-17**

Use this idea to remind your people how easy serving others can be.

(continued on p. 49)

ACTS OF SERVICE

Directions: Photocopy and cut apart this handout for use during the "May I Be of Service?" idea.

● Check to find what the next song will be. Look this up in a song book and mark it for someone.

● Look for someone you haven't met before. Introduce yourself.

● Give a 60-second shoulder massage to someone.

● Greet someone warmly and tell that person one reason why you're glad he or she is here today.

● Ask someone how you can be praying for him or her. Commit to praying for that person for the next three days.

Photocopy the "Acts of Service" handout on page 48 and cut it into the indicated strips. You'll need to make enough strips so each person in the congregation can have one. Fold these and divide them among the offering plates.

At the appropriate time during your sermon, have ushers pass the plates and ask each person to remove one slip of paper.

Say: **It's one thing to talk about service. But it's another thing to actually serve. Let's practice putting Jesus' message in John 13:1-17 into action by doing these simple acts of service for the next 60 seconds. You may serve anyone in the room. Ready? Go.**

After everyone has completed an act of service and returned to his or her seat, say: **Let's remember how easy it is to follow Jesus' example of service. Hopefully these small acts of kindness will challenge us to look for other opportunities to serve others in little or big ways this week.**

Continue with your sermon.

Pass the Hat

TOPIC: SHOWING RESPECT TO ALL PEOPLE

SCRIPTURE: JAMES 2:1-17

This sermon idea reminds us that God wants us to love and honor everyone, not just the rich or those with prestigious positions.

You'll need to gather four hats that represent different vocations, such as a firefighter's helmet, a nurse's cap, a cowboy hat, and a construction worker's hard hat. Borrow hats from people in your congregation, or check a local toy store for inexpensive hats to use.

When you're ready for this part of your sermon, invite four volunteers from the congregation to join you at the pulpit. Do not try to match volunteers to hats that would represent their real careers. Place one of your career hats on each volunteer.

Next, have congregation members form groups of no more than four and discuss impressions a stranger might have of the volunteers. For example, a person wearing a firefighter's hat might be seen as brave, a person wearing a nurse's hat might be viewed as caring, a person wearing a cowboy hat might enjoy adventure, and a person wearing a construction worker's hard hat might be con-

What makes a sermon memorable for me is . . .
"When the speaker really gets the point across in an interesting way."

sidered strong. Then have the foursomes tell how a stranger would act toward the volunteers. For example, a firefighter might be given a lot of respect and honor, while the construction worker might be ignored as a common laborer.

Have the person in each foursome who has worked the longest at his or her current job report answers to the entire congregation. (You may want to limit the number of reports from foursomes to accommodate your time.)

Finally, allow volunteers to tell their names and one or two facts about themselves, such as hobbies they enjoy or things they like to do in their spare time. Compare their information with the impressions of the congregation.

Then say: **As we can see from our volunteers, outward appearances can be misleading. At best, they give only a hint of what's inside. At worst, they mask a person completely. Unfortunately, we often give or withhold honor from others based on their appearances or the types of job they have. James 2 helps us discover what God thinks of this kind of behavior.**

Thank your volunteers and allow them to return to their seats, then continue with your sermon.

HIGH
MEDIUM
LOW

RISK RATING

Position of Prayer

TOPIC: INTERCEDING ON BEHALF OF OTHERS

SCRIPTURE: PHILEMON 4-21

Use this physical prayer picture to bring home the news that just as Paul interceded on behalf of the runaway slave, Onesimus, we can offer prayer on behalf of others in need.

After explaining Paul's efforts on behalf of Onesimus, a slave in need, have everyone stand for prayer. Explain that you're going to be allowing a few minutes for people to pray silently about specific needs. Then say: **Bow your head and pray for those in the world who are oppressed. Include those unable to worship freely, those who are terrorized by more powerful groups, and those who cannot hold their heads high and walk in freedom.**

Allow a moment for people to pray, then continue: **Now sit down and pray for those who are unable to stand, those who** have disabilities, and people who are challenged physically, mentally, emotionally, or in other ways.

After a few minutes say: **Now kneel (bend down) where you are and pray for the small people of the world—children. Pray for their hearts to be turned to Jesus, that their parents or other adults will love them, and for their health and education.**

Again allow time for silent prayer, then continue: **Put your face as close to the ground as possible and pray for those who are weak and those who cannot pray for themselves. Pray for those who are sick, in hospitals, and those unborn.**

After a few minutes say: **Remain in this position and thank God for every opportunity you've had to show love to a person who was weak or without a voice.**

Continue: **Now return to your kneeling position and offer thanks for the children God has put in your life—your own children or younger relatives, children of your friends or the children in your neighborhood. Thank God for giving you the opportunity to show his love to these little ones.**

Allow time for thanks, then say: **Return to your seat, and as you sit, thank God for your life. No matter how frail and imperfect our bodies are, we have been given eternal life in Jesus. Thank God for that.**

After a moment of thanks continue: **Now stand with your head bowed and thank God for the freedom you have. Even if you feel oppressed in some part of your life, you have freedom from sin in Jesus. Thank God for his mercy and forgiveness.**

Close this time of prayer by asking God to help the people of your church remember to pray for those in need. Then continue your sermon.

Salt and Light

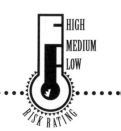

TOPIC: WE ARE SALT AND LIGHT TO THE WORLD
SCRIPTURE: MATTHEW 5:13-16

Use this activity to help congregation members better understand the concept of being salt and light to the world. You'll need to purchase salt packets, such as the kind used in fast-food restaurants, for this activity. (Your church kitchen may already have a supply, or you may want to check a restaurant supply company or grocery warehouse.)

Have everyone form groups of up to three people. Have ushers give each group on the left side of the church a packet of salt.

Say: **I'd like those groups with salt to examine it and discuss everything you know or can discover about salt. For example, you might say, "Salt tastes bad by itself but is good when used to season food" or "It takes thousands of salt crystals to create a salty taste."**

Turn to the groups on the right side of the church and say: **Those of you without salt will be examining the light in this room. Share everything you know or can discover about light. For example, you might say, "We need light to see, but too much light can blind us."**

Allow several minutes for group discussion. Then have each "salt" person find a "light" person and form pairs. If you have more of one group than the other, let extra people join pairs to form trios.

Say: **Tell your new partner everything you learned in your previous group.**

After a moment of sharing, say: **Now that you know all there is to know about salt and light, discuss with your partner the qualities of salt and light that a Christian might also have.**

After several minutes of discussion, invite the person wearing the most buttons in each pair to report any insights gained through this discussion. Have as many people share as time allows, then continue your sermon.

Sunday with Meraldo

TOPIC: JUDGING OTHERS

SCRIPTURE: LUKE 6:39-49

Use this skit as a discussion starter during a sermon on the dangers of judging by outward appearances.

A few weeks ahead of time, recruit seven people to perform the skit. Give each person a photocopy of the skit and arrange for the group to rehearse at least once before the actual performance.

After the skit, have congregation members find partners to discuss these questions:

(continued on p. 56)

SUNDAY WITH MERALDO

The Scene: This skit takes place on a fictitious talk show similar to "Donahue." Have the three guests, Bill, Sue, and Roger, seated in chairs on the stage. The host will need a microphone that can be moved throughout the congregation. For the ease of the host, have the three persons who will be asking questions sit on aisles where the microphone can easily reach.

CHARACTERS

Meraldo: Talk show host. (Or Soaprah Raphael if host is a woman.)

Brother Bill: Male Christian with a stuffy personality. Should wear suit and tie. Have Bill reverently holding a large Bible on his lap. (A dictionary or other large book will work as well.) Before the skit, generously sprinkle baby powder or corn starch on the top of the book. (This will serve as dust.)

Sister Sue: Female Christian with a socialite personality. Should wear fancy dress, gloves, and hat if possible.

Roger: Regular guy. Should wear neat but casual clothes.

Audience Member #1: Person in congregation who asks a scripted question. Can go by his or her real name.

Audience Member #2: Person in congregation who asks a scripted question. Can go by his or her real name.

Audience Member #3: Person in congregation who asks a scripted question. Can go by his or her real name.

(Note: For added humor have Bill and Sue ad-lib saying "Amen," "Praise God," and "Hallelujah," after each other's answers.)

•••

(Scene opens with jazzy intro music. Meraldo walks quickly onto stage and begins speaking.)

Meraldo: Welcome to "Sunday," the talk show for Christians. I'm your host, Meraldo Ronahue, and today we are proud to bring you our show from *(name your location)*. On our show today we'll be interviewing three Christians to determine how to judge what a true Christian is really like. Our panel is made up of Christians from *(name your church)*. Let me introduce Brother Bill! *(Bill nods, then seriously blows a cloud of "dust" off the top of his Bible.)* Sister Sue! *(Sue waves graciously.)* And Roger! *(Roger nods and smiles.)* Now, let's get some questions from the audience about how to judge a true Christian. *(Goes to Audience Member #1.)* Yes, what's your question?

Audience Member #1: Let's say it's Wednesday evening, and I'm about to leave for my bowling league. I get a flat tire. Which of you would help me change it?

Brother Bill: You could borrow my jack if you needed to. I'd assist you myself if I weren't on my way out to do door-to-door evangelism in our neighborhood. Evangelism is very important for the truly spiritual. You see . . . my tie would probably get grease on it, and that would look tacky to potential new Christians.

Sister Sue: Well, I'd really like to, but Wednesday night I have prayer meeting. Others might talk if I got there late, so I wouldn't be able to help you. Of course I'd be glad to call the auto club for you.

Roger: I'd be glad to change it. Then we could drive over to get the flat repaired together. You know, I like to bowl a little myself. Maybe I could join—

Meraldo: *(Cutting off Roger)* Well, those are some great answers! Let's get another question from our studio audience. *(Moves to second audience member.)* And what is your question?

Audience Member #2: Here's the situation. I have to stay home from work one day with the flu. Would any of you Christians be able to drive my daughter to school?

Brother Bill: I'd be happy to, except my son goes to a different school than your daughter so it's too far out of my way. I have my son in a Christian school, you know. He's going to be a missionary when he grows up. Save the natives from the devil and all that, you know.

Sister Sue: I couldn't do it because I'd be late for morning Bible study at the church. I wouldn't normally mind being a FEW minutes late, but it IS my week to bring doughnuts, and no one would understand the doughnuts being late. *(Shrugs.)*

Roger: Hey, don't worry about it. I can drop your daughter off at school. Then, if you like, I can stop by the store on my way back and pick up some ginger ale and hot soup for you.

Meraldo: Well, that's wonderful. What a great Christian! Let's see if we can get one more question. *(Moves to third audience member.)* Good morning, what would you like to ask our panel?

Audience Member #3: My wife and I always enjoy the annual block party. Will any of you Christians be able to join us this year?

Brother Bill: Hmm . . . Seems to me that always falls on a Saturday afternoon. That's right when I'm preparing for my Sunday school lesson. It takes awhile to look up every Scripture in the Greek or Hebrew, you know. Then there are all the commentaries I have to consult—that takes time. It's important for a real Christian to take Bible study seriously, so I'm afraid I'll have to skip the party. Again.

Sister Sue: I don't mean to sound like a goody-two-shoes or anything *(giggles)*, but there'll be beer at the party. What WILL the ladies advisory council say if they hear I've been at a party where alcohol was served? No, I don't think it would be the best thing for my Christian image. You'll have to count me out.

Roger: Block party, huh? That sounds like fun! Think we could get a volleyball game going?

Meraldo: *(Jumping in)* Well, time's up for today. I'd like to thank our panel. With answers like these it would be difficult for me to say which of you is or isn't a true Christian. I'm just curious about one thing, though. Would each of you tell the audience how long you've been a Christian?

Brother Bill: Certainly! I've been saved, saved, saved for 21 years!

Sister Sue: I was "born again" 12 years ago!

Roger: *(Scratching his head)* Well, to tell you the truth, I'm not a Christian. I'm the janitor at the church. Some guy called and said he couldn't make it today because he had a Sunday school board meeting. I figured I'd just fill in for him and help out.

Meraldo: *(Cutting Roger off and very embarrassed)* Uhhh—yeah. Well, that's all for today, see you next week on "Sunday" with Meraldo! *(Under his breath)* Why do these things always happen to me?

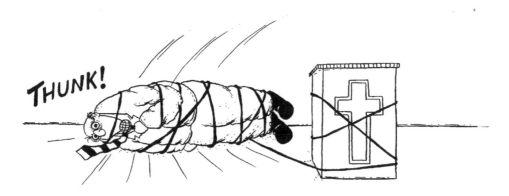

THIS INCIDENT PRETTY MUCH CONVINCED THE
CONGREGATION TO PITCH IN AND GET PASTOR MENLEY
A CORDLESS MICROPHONE.

● Which character in the skit could you best identify with? Why?

● Describe a time you misjudged someone based on his or her outward appearance.

● What's one important thing this skit brought to your mind about judging others?

After a time of discussion, continue with your sermon.

The Eyes Have It

TOPIC: SHARING YOUR FAITH WITH OTHERS
SCRIPTURE: ROMANS 10:8-18

Use this idea during a sermon to demonstrate the many ways we share our faith.

Have everyone form pairs and stand facing each other. Have each pair designate one partner to be A and one to be B.

Say: **Let's have the B's go first. I'd like you to use your eyes to communicate a message to your partner. You may want to express an emotion, your thoughts about this sermon, or any other message that comes to mind. Remember to use only your eyes.**

Allow a moment for the B's to send their messages while the A's guess what the messages are. Then have partners switch roles and repeat the experience with the A's sending the message.

Next, have each pair join with another pair to form groups of four to discuss the following questions (allow about a minute for groups to discuss each question):

● What was easy or hard for you about this assignment?

● How did you use your eyes to communicate your message?

● We communicate our faith in Christ to others in more ways than just the words we speak. How can we make that communication as clear and unmistakable as possible?

If you like, have members of different groups share answers to the last question with the entire congregation. Then continue your sermon.

I'd like to see my pastor try some new methods other than lecture because . . . "Creativity increases memory."

The "Loving Your Enemies Little Instruction Book"

TOPIC: LOVE YOUR ENEMIES

SCRIPTURE: MATTHEW 5:38-48

Loving your enemies is a great idea—in theory. But how do you help your congregation go beyond theory and put into practice Jesus' command in Matthew 5:38-48? Why not compile a "Loving Your Enemies Little Instruction Book" to allow congregation members to give each other practical, specific advice for how to apply Jesus' words?

Near the end of your sermon on this topic, say: **H. Jackson Brown Jr. has had immense success selling a book called** *Life's Little Instruction Book.* **In this book, he simply lists hundreds of bits of wisdom and advice for living.**

Let's create our congregation's own "Loving Your Enemies Little Instruction Book." With this book we can share practical advice for how to apply Jesus' words from Matthew 5:38-48 in our everyday lives.

Have congregation members pause for a moment to think of one specific word of wisdom or advice telling how to show love to an enemy. Spark ideas by asking the congregation to think in terms of things they could do this week at home, work, the gym, political meetings, while shopping, and so on.

Next, have ushers distribute 3×5 cards to everyone in the congregation. Ask people to write their thoughts on how to love enemies on their cards.

Remind listeners to be specific in the things they write. For example, someone's advice might be, "No matter how awful you consider your daughter's boyfriend to be, invite him to dinner and be polite during the entire meal." Or "Leave a candy bar on the desk of an associate you're not getting along with."

After everyone has had time to write his or her ideas, have ushers gather the cards. During the week, read through and eliminate only inappropriate ideas. Have a volunteer type up the ideas into a master copy. Then photocopy or have printed enough copies of your master for everyone in the congregation. Include a cover page titled, "(Name of Your Church)'s Loving Your Enemies Little Instruction Book."

One encouraging thought I'd like to share with people who deliver sermons is . . . "People really do listen and want to love Jesus better."

The next week, pass out copies of your newly created instruction book as people come in for the worship service. Encourage people to read the ideas in the book and to put them to use over the next two weeks. You might want to take time in a few weeks to hear the results of some of these actions!

HIGH
MEDIUM
LOW

RISK RATING

The Other Santa Sack

TOPIC: HELPING OTHERS

SCRIPTURE: GALATIANS 6:1-10, focusing on verses 2, 9-10

Use this idea to give people an opportunity to take their faith out of the pew and into the world.

About a week before using this idea, informally poll members to find out specific needs in your church. Perhaps a family is in need of winter clothes, someone may need meals delivered during an illness, or a Sunday school class may be in need of a teacher. Then gather items to represent each of these needs.

For example, a mitten could represent the need for winter clothes, a paper plate could represent the need for meals, and a curriculum book might represent the need for a teacher. Attach a 3×5 card to each item telling the details of the specific need. Place all these items in a pillowcase.

During your sermon, sling the pillowcase over your shoulder and walk into the congregation. Continue with your sermon for several minutes without offering any explanation for the sack or your actions.

Then say: **We've all heard of Santa's bag of goodies, but maybe you haven't heard of the other Santa sack. This burden I'm carrying doesn't contain toys for good little boys and girls. It's filled with opportunities for us to put our faith into action and fulfill the instructions we've read in Galatians 6.**

Remove each item from the pillowcase and describe the need it represents. Then encourage members to take the items after the service to signify their commitment to meeting the needs represented.

Finish by offering brief prayers of support for those who choose to help meet the needs.

Variation: To bring home the immediacy of the need, ask for a volunteer from the congregation to commit right away after describing an item from the Santa sack. Give the volunteer the item to keep as a reminder of his or her commitment. Continue the process until you've gone through all the items in the sack. If no one volunteers for a particular item, return it to the sack.

Time With a Child

HIGH
MEDIUM
LOW

RISK RATING

TOPIC: RELATIONSHIPS WITH CHILDREN
SCRIPTURE: MARK 10:13-16

Use this idea to help your congregation follow the example of Jesus' love for children.

Photocopy the coupons on the "Coupon for Kids" handout (p. 61) and place one coupon in each copy of your worship-service bulletin. Have a stack of extra coupons available for people who need more than one.

As you discuss the actions of Jesus in Mark 10, ask the members of the congregation to take the coupons from their bulletins.

Say: **Children were and are important to Jesus. He went out of his way to spend time with them. And we can do that, too. To help us commit to following Jesus' example, I've prepared these coupons to give to the special children in our lives. Let's take a moment to fill these out right now.**

Guide congregation members as they fill out their coupons. First, have each person think of a child he or she would like to do something special for and write that child's name in the appropriate spot on the coupon. Encourage parents to give a coupon to each of their children. (Have ushers or assistants ready with extra coupons for those who need them.) Encourage people without children at home to choose another child, such as a grandchild, niece or nephew, younger brother or sister, or child of a close friend or co-worker.

Next, have everyone fill in an activity to do with the child to make that child feel special. Remind people to think of the child's interests, not just their own. You might suggest activities such as the following to spark people's thinking:

● dinner or dessert at the place of the child's choice;

- miniature golf;
- playing catch (or another sport or game) for an hour;
- going window shopping;
- going to the library, then curling up with hot chocolate while the older person reads aloud to the child;
- a trip to the park (with the adult playing on the playground equipment too, not merely watching the child!);
- an attempt to build the world's largest banana split;
- an evening of playing the child's favorite board games;
- a trip to a sporting event the child enjoys; or
- a camping or hiking trip.

Finally, have everyone sign and date each coupon. Encourage congregation members to deliver their coupons during the next seven days.

As you wrap up your sermon, challenge people to think about Jesus' example in Mark 10:13-16 during their time with their chosen children. Ask: **Why does Jesus say we must be like children to enter God's kingdom? What about children is so appealing to Jesus?**

Variation: Distribute lollipops and ribbons that can be tied to the coupons as an extra treat for the children receiving them.

I NEVER THOUGHT PROMISING TO SHORTEN MY SERMON WOULD AFFECT THE OFFERING.

COUPON FOR KIDS!

To _____

This coupon good for _____

With love _____

(No expiration date)

COUPON FOR KIDS!

To _____

This coupon good for _____

With love _____

(No expiration date)

We're in This Together!

TOPIC: CHRISTIAN COMMUNITY

SCRIPTURE: ACTS 2:36-47

Acts 2:36-47 describes how the first Christians were eager to share finances, food, homes, and other resources with each other. Try this activity to give your church members a chance to experience the joy of sharing God's physical blessings.

After you've discussed Acts 2:36-47 in your sermon, distribute 3×5 cards. Have people write their names, addresses, and phone numbers on one side of their cards.

Then say: **I'd like us all to have the opportunity to share our resources with each other like the early Christians did. On the blank side of your card, write one resource you have that you'd be willing to share with one other person in our congregation.**

For example, you may have a piano that a child could practice on twice a week. You may have gardening space to share with an apartment-bound person. Perhaps you have a lawn mower another person could borrow, or maybe there's a spare shelf in your freezer for someone to store a summer vegetable crop.

Remind people that what they offer doesn't need to be something big such as offering to chauffeur children to school each day. It can simply be sharing what they have. Also, make sure people understand that the things they're offering only need to be shared with one other person.

When everyone has completed his or her card, collect the cards. Choose an easily accessible spot to place or post the cards. Tell people where the cards will be. Then say: **If you have a need that you think someone in the church could meet, take a moment to look over these cards. If you see a card offering to share something you can use, take the card and contact the person who wrote it. We'll keep the cards out for the next three weeks.**

Continue with your sermon. After the service, have several assistants place or post the cards in your designated area. After three weeks, remove any remaining cards and keep them at the church office. You never know when someone may call in need of something another can offer!

VIEW FROM THE PEW

I'd like to see my pastor try some new methods other than lecture because . . .
"It is fun to do something different once in a while."

Sermon Ideas About

Christian Concerns

About That Debt...

TOPIC: FORGIVENESS

SCRIPTURE: MATTHEW 18:21-35

Use this creative reading based on Jesus' parable about forgiveness in Matthew 18:21-35 to open or close your sermon in a dramatic way. Make photocopies of the script on pages 65-66 and select five people to practice it in the weeks before your sermon.

At the appropriate time during your sermon, invite your readers to the pulpit area. Have them stand in a row and read the script aloud in a creative and dramatic way. If possible, have a microphone available for each reader.

After the reading, thank your readers and continue your sermon.

A Cookie to the Wise

TOPIC: WISDOM

SCRIPTURE: JAMES 3:13-18

Use this idea during your sermon to compare God's wisdom to the world's wisdom. You'll need enough fortune cookies for each person in your congregation to have one. Fortune cookies are available at most grocery stores, but if you need a large supply, you might check a few local Chinese restaurants or warehouse food stores.

After you've discussed James 3:13-18 in your sermon, have ushers distribute the fortune cookies, one to each congregation member.

Say: **Break open your cookie and read the enclosed fortune.**

Invite anyone who thinks their fortune is funny, or in some way inappropriate, to share this with the entire congregation. Wait for several to share.

(continued on p. 67)

CREATIVE READING FOR MATTHEW 18:21-35

Reader 1: Then Peter came to Jesus and asked,

Reader 2: Lord, when my fellow believer sins against me, how many times must I forgive him? Should I forgive him as many as seven times?

Reader 1: Jesus answered,

Reader 2: I tell you, you must forgive him more than seven times. You must forgive him even if he does wrong to you 77 times.

Reader 1: The kingdom of heaven is like a king who decided to collect the money his servants owed him. When the king began to collect his money, a servant who owed him several million dollars was brought to him.

Reader 3: *(Pretending to talk on the phone)* Mrs. Johnson? Your son just blew up the entire science lab . . . of course, you'll be held responsible for the damages . . .

Reader 4: *(Pretending to read a letter)* Dear Citizen: The IRS has determined your taxes are equal to the entire national debt.

Reader 5: *(As if talking to spouse)* You charged HOW much on our credit card?

Reader 2: But the servant did not have enough money to pay his master, the king.

Reader 3: I'm broke!

Reader 4: I'll never have that much money!

Reader 5: *(Slapping hand against cheek with expression of terror)* AAAAGGGHHH!

Reader 1: So the master ordered that everything the servant owned should be sold,

Readers 3,4,5: Everything?

Reader 1: Even the servant's wife and children. Then the money would be used to pay the king what the servant owed. But the servant fell on his knees and begged,

Readers 3,4,5: *(Falling to knees and folding hands as if pleading)* Be patient with me, and I will pay you everything I owe.

Reader 2: The master felt sorry for his servant and told him he did not have to pay it back. Then he let the servant go free.

Reader 3: Debt canceled!

Reader 5: No more collection agents!

Reader 4: Get out of jail free!

Reader 1: Later, that same servant found another servant who owed him a few dollars. The servant grabbed him around the neck and said, "Pay me the money you owe me!"

Reader 3: Um, about that lunch you borrowed money for last week . . .

CREATIVE READING FOR MATTHEW 18:21-35
(CONTINUED)

Reader 4: *(Angrily)* Your kid stepped on my prize daisies! I expect IMMEDIATE restitution!

Reader 5: *(Rolling up sleeves as if ready to fight)* You scratched the fender on my 1973 sporty red Pinto station wagon! I'll fix you!

Reader 2: The other servant fell on his knees and begged him, "Be patient with me, and I will pay you everything I owe!"

Readers 3,4,5: *(Arms crossed and tapping feet)* But the first servant refused to be patient.

Reader 1: He threw the other servant into prison until he could pay everything he owed.

Reader 2: When the other servants saw what had happened, they were very sorry.

Reader 1: So they went and told their master all that had happened.

Reader 2: Then the master called his servant in and said, "You evil servant! Because you begged me to forget what you owed, I told you that you did not have to pay anything. You should have showed mercy to that other servant, just as I showed mercy to you."

Readers 3,4,5: *(Hang heads in shame and stay that way until last line of skit.)*

Reader 1: The master was very angry and put the servant in prison to be punished until he could pay everything he owed.

Reader 2: *(In a deadpan voice)* Go directly to jail. Do not pass Go. Do not collect $200.

Reader 1: This king did what my heavenly Father will do to us

Reader 2: if we do not forgive our brother

Reader 1: or sister

All: from our hearts.

Then have congregation members find a partner to discuss these questions:

- If you were to write a "fortune" based on James 3:13-18, what would it say?
- How does worldly wisdom, as we've seen in these fortune cookies, compare to God's wisdom, as we've read in James 3:13-18?

Have several people share any insights they gained from their discussions. Then continue your sermon. You may also want to compare God's wisdom to other sources of worldly wisdom such as horoscopes, the media, and so on.

Against the Flow

TOPIC: IN THE WORLD BUT NOT OF IT
SCRIPTURE: JOHN 17:1-26

Use this activity to demonstrate the difficulty we face living in the world without being a part of it.

Plan to have the congregation sing a song just before your sermon. Before that song, have people in each pew or row number off from one to four. Then say: **Let's all stand for this song. But I'd like all the "fours" to turn and face the back of the room while we sing.**

These people don't need to move anywhere, just turn and face the back. Most of them will end up looking into the face of the person standing behind them. Continue with the singing in this manner.

When the singing is over, have everyone sit down and allow those who were facing the back to return to their normal positions. Then have everyone form groups of up to four with those around them, including at least one "four" in each group. Ask those who had to face the back to share what feelings they had while singing. Have others in the groups tell what they were thinking about during the whole experience.

After a few moments for discussion, invite representatives from several groups to report the results of their discussions to the congregation.

Then say: **When singers were facing the back, it was obvious they were going against the flow. In a simple way, this illustrates** the stress of what it's like to be in the world, but not a part of it. Jesus knew living in the world and not being of it would be tough at times. But we can be encouraged by Jesus' prayer of strength for us as we go against the tide of the world.

Continue your sermon, reading John 17:1-26 and offering encouragement for those who feel pressured by the world to go in the wrong direction.

Appeal for Those in Authority

TOPIC: PRAYER FOR LEADERS
SCRIPTURE: 1 TIMOTHY 2:1-4

Use this prayer activity to help members of your congregation put into practice the instructions of 1 Timothy 2:1-4.

You'll need to prepare for this several weeks ahead of time. Using the letter below as a guide, write letters to a variety of leaders in your community, state, and nation.

> Dear _____:
>
> As responsible citizens, and in response to the Bible's teaching in 1 Timothy 2:1-4, the members of our church, (name of our church), would like to pray for you.
>
> We would like our prayers to address your specific needs. If you'd like us to pray in specific ways for you, please send a quick letter telling us how we can pray for you. We've enclosed a self-addressed, stamped envelope for your convenience. We plan to have a time of prayer for your request(s) on (date), so please be prompt with your reply.
>
> Thank you!
>
> (Your name, title, church name, and address)

Offer to pray for your chosen leaders. Don't use the letters to preach politics and don't ask for anything in return, because that could make the leaders distrust your motives. Give the leaders at least two to three weeks to respond. Send these letters to leaders in your church, city council members, state senators, popular musicians, famous actors and actresses, even leaders on the national level. You'll probably need to send 30 or more letters to get a good number of responses (the more you send, the better response you'll get). Include a stamped, self-addressed return envelope to encourage a prompt response.

After you have received a good number of responses (10 or more), compile the information onto one or two pages. For example, you might write something like:

- Our city planner, Rachel Gutierrez, requests prayer for. . . .
- Anthony Hassen, an elder in our church, requests prayer for. . .
- Ron Stinnett, popular Christian musician, requests prayer for. . .
- Governor Wakefield requests prayer for. . .

and so on.

Take this list of requests, photocopy it, and cut the copies so that each slip of paper has one request on it. Make enough copies of the original list so each member of your congregation can have at least one slip with a request on it. This will mean several people will have the same request, but that's OK.

Have ushers distribute the slips of paper at the appropriate time during the sermon.

Say: **I'd like us to do more than simply hear the instructions of 1 Timothy 2:1-4; I want us to put God's Word into practice. So I've contacted a variety of leaders in our church, community, and nation and asked for specific ways we can pray for them. Right now, read the prayer request on the slip of paper you received. Then silently pray for this person and his or her request for one minute.**

Allow a minute for silent prayer. Then have each person trade slips of paper with another person sitting nearby. Again, have a minute of silent prayer. Have everyone trade his or her prayer request slip twice more, each time allowing a minute for prayer.

Afterward, encourage each person to take a slip of paper home and commit to praying for this request three more times in the coming week. Then continue your sermon.

What I like least about sermons is . . . "The same format week after week."

"I HAVE NOTICED THAT THE CONGREGATION OFTEN PAYS MORE ATTENTION TO THE CHILDREN'S SERMON THAN THE REGULAR SERMON. SO TODAY WE'RE GOING TO TRY SOMETHING NEW . . ."

Determining the Truth

TOPIC: FALSE TEACHING
SCRIPTURE: 2 JOHN 7-11

Use this idea to help people determine how they decide whether or not something is true and to explore biblical guidelines for evaluating the teachings they hear.

During your sermon, read the following statements aloud. Have everyone stand who believes a statement is true. Those believing a statement is false should remain seated. After everyone has shown an opinion, tell whether the statement is true or false. Here are the statements:

● **When all his teammates fouled out of the game, high school basketball player Pat McGee finished the game for his school alone—and won.** (True. This happened in 1937 at St. Peter's High School.)

● **In the late 1800s, a sailor who was lost at sea was found later that day, alive, in the belly of a whale his shipmates had killed.** (True.)

● **No one was able to go over Niagara Falls and live to tell about it until Annie Taylor did it in 1951.** (False. Annie Taylor actually did this in 1901. And just a sidelight—she couldn't swim!)

● **Napoleon Bonaparte once tried to poison himself because he lost a battle.** (True. However, the poison gave him hiccups, which forced the poison out of his stomach.)

● **Actor Harrison Ford got the trademark scar under his lip while filming the movie, _Star Wars._** (False. He drove into a tree while trying to buckle his seat belt.)

Have everyone return to his or her seat and find a partner. Have partners discuss these questions:

● **How did you decide what was true or false during this quiz?**

● **How do you decide what's true and what's false in your day-to-day life?**

After discussion, allow several people to share their thoughts. Then continue your sermon, using 2 John 7-11 to explain John's criteria for determining what is true or false. Encourage your congregation members to follow John's teaching in determining what's true today.

Gift of Hope

HIGH
MEDIUM
LOW

RISK RATING

TOPIC: THE HOPE OF ETERNITY WITH GOD
SCRIPTURE: REVELATION 21:1-6

The hope of heaven is one of the greatest things Christians have. To illustrate this, find a very large box such as a refrigerator box. Place an insignificant item (such as an old sock) in the box and tie a huge bow around the box. (If you have enough paper, you could gift-wrap the box as well!) Place this beside the pulpit or speaking area. Don't let your congregation see you carry it in.

As you begin your sermon, have people join with two others to form trios.

Say: **Imagine that this box could contain *anything* in the world. What would you hope to find when you opened this box?**

Have trios discuss the question. Then have the person in each group wearing the most buttons share the group's favorite response. Allow as many to share as you have time for.

Then have a volunteer come forward to open the box. After showing the contents to the congregation, ask: **How did the contents of this box match with your expectations?**

Afterward say: **It's fun at times to hope for anything in the world. But our worldly hopes often end in disappointment. Revelation 21:1-6 describes a hope for Christians that's out of this world (and that won't disappoint). It's bigger and more impressive than anything a box like this could ever hold—it's a new heaven and earth. The physical presence of God. No tears, no death, no sadness, no crying or pain for the rest of eternity. Let's learn more about this hope of eternity Christians can have.**

Continue with your sermon, comparing the hopes we have in this life to the incredible hope of eternal life in the presence of God.

VIEW FROM THE PEW

I'd like to see my pastor try some new methods other than lecture because . . .
"The change could bring more life in the service."

Hidden Gifts

TOPIC: SPIRITUAL GIFTS

SCRIPTURE: ROMANS 12:1-16

Many people think they simply don't have anything to offer the Christian community. Use this idea to demonstrate to your congregation just how many gifts God has given your church.

You'll need enough uninflated balloons for each person to have one and markers that can be shared. Distribute the balloons as people enter the room, or place several balloons and one or two markers at the end of each row.

During your sermon, after you've discussed the variety of spiritual gifts mentioned in Romans 12:1-16, have everyone blow up and tie the balloons.

Say: **On your balloon, write one spiritual gift you believe God has given you. Use the gifts we've discussed today as a guide. For example, you might write "Serving" or "Teaching."** You don't need to write your name or anything else, just a gift you think God has given you. If you don't know what your gift might be, list one of your talents or abilities.

After everyone has done this, say: **When I give the signal, toss your balloon up into the air and bat it away from you. Then catch a different balloon. Go!**

When the air has cleared of balloons say: **Now read what's written on your balloon. If the balloon you caught has the gift of "teaching" on it, stand and hold up the balloon.**

Have these people remain standing, then go through the rest of the gifts listed in Romans 12:1-16 and have people holding balloons for each gift join the others already standing.

When everyone is standing with a balloon, say: **You may not have thought you had much to offer, but look at all the gifts that are hidden in our congregation!**

Have everyone sit down, then continue your sermon explaining how to use spiritual gifts so they won't be hidden from others in your congregation. Offer specific ways people with different gifts can use them in your church and community.

VIEW FROM THE PEW

One encouraging thought I'd like to share with people who deliver sermons is . . . "A good sermon will last me all week, even months. I appreciate the time spent in preparing them."

Hot Shots

HIGH
MEDIUM
LOW

RISK RATING

TOPIC: LIVING BY FAITH

SCRIPTURE: 2 CORINTHIANS 4:13-18

Use this idea to help people understand that we can have faith in God because God never fails.

During your sermon, place an empty trash can or bucket about 10 feet from where you are standing. Hold up a paper wad and explain that you're going to throw it into the can.

Say: **If you think I can do this in one shot, stand up now to show your faith in me.**

After people stand (if any!), have them be seated again. Then ask congregation members who have faith in you to make the shot in two tries to stand. When these people have shown their opinion, have them return to their seats. Next, ask people who don't think you'll be able to make the shot in less than three tries to stand. Have everyone sit down and take your shot (or shots!).

Afterward say: **You all had different levels of faith in my ability. I can't blame you because my abilities are undependable. But we *can* have complete faith in God, because God never fails.**

Continue with your sermon, emphasizing the idea that only God is completely trustworthy.

AFTER THE SLIDE PROJECTOR BROKE, PASTOR
SPACKLEY'S VISUAL PRESENTATIONS TO THE BOARD
TOOK A DRASTIC TURN FOR THE WORSE.

Just a Minute

TOPIC: PATIENCE

SCRIPTURE: JAMES 5:7-11

What better way to illustrate patience than to make your congregation wait! Begin your sermon in this way...

When it's time for you to speak, take your time walking up to the pulpit. Dawdle for at least three full minutes before beginning to speak. Here are some ideas to fill those three minutes:

● Stop to chat for a moment with the music director or a person sitting near the front on an aisle.

● Take off a jacket or sweater and carefully fold, refold, then place on a seat nearby.

● Adjust the microphone, taking great pains to get it just right.

● Look for your pen.

● Rummage through your notes.

● Reset your watch.

When you feel like congregation members have squirmed long enough, say: **I hope you're not in a hurry! Turn to the person next to you and share what you were thinking or feeling as I seemingly wasted time up here.**

After a minute or two of discussion time, say: **Now tell your partner what things in real life bring out feelings of impatience in you.**

Allow another minute or two for discussion, then have a few people call out their responses for the whole congregation.

Continue your sermon, including discussion of patience on a day-to-day basis and being patient in waiting for Christ's return.

Key to Riches

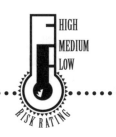

HIGH
MEDIUM
LOW

RISK RATING

TOPIC: TRUE RICHES

SCRIPTURE: 1 TIMOTHY 6:6-16

This idea demonstrates the best "Get Rich Quick" scheme ever invented!

You'll need an empty soft drink bottle, a treasure map (directions are given below), and a large key cut out of cardboard. Cover the key with foil or spray paint it a metallic color. Attach a note to the key with 1 Timothy 6:6 written out on it. Then hide the key under a pew or seat so that it won't be seen by those sitting near it.

Prepare a treasure map with directions such as these:

THE KEY TO RICHES BEYOND YOUR WILDEST DREAMS!

Find a person wearing red. Move three people to the left. Go two rows back. Go to the closest person wearing glasses. Move one row forward, then take five giant steps toward the center of the building. Go to the closest person with a birthday in this month. Look under that person's seat for a treasure.

Roll up the directions to the treasure and place the paper in the soft drink bottle. (To make it easier to remove the paper, leave a bit of the paper sticking out of the bottle's neck.) Then take the bottle with you as you walk up to the pulpit to begin your sermon.

Say: **It's been really hard for me to keep my mind on today's sermon because I recently found this bottle with a note inside.** Hold up the bottle. **I hope no one minds, but I just have to see what it says.** Remove the paper from the bottle and begin reading. **"The Key to Riches Beyond Your Wildest Dreams." Why, it's a treasure map! Let's see where it leads!**

Begin reading the directions aloud and follow them one direction at a time. Add to the excitement by actually climbing over the pews or chairs, walking down the rows, standing in front of specified persons, and so on. When you arrive at the designated person, look under that seat. Most likely the treasure (the key) won't be there, so say: **It's not here! Maybe I misread the directions. But the treasure must be under another seat. Everyone look under your seat for the treasure!**

When someone finds the key, take it to the front of the church and read the attached Scripture passage aloud. Say: **The treasure map was right about one thing: Serving God is the key to treasure beyond anyone's wildest dreams.** Then continue your sermon, explaining how serving God, not money, is what makes us truly rich.

TODAY'S SERVICE WILL BE IN 3-D.

HIGH
MEDIUM
LOW

RISK RATING

Multiplied Talents

TOPIC: USING GOD'S GIFTS
SCRIPTURE: LUKE 19:11-27

In April 1991, Charisma magazine reported an unusual happening. Instead of asking his congregation for money, Pastor Phil Derstine had given $5 each to 250 members of his church. These people had 30 days to follow the example of Luke 19:11-27 and multiply this gift. At the end of the month, the $1,250 investment came back as

$10,000! Derstine's illustration was certainly risky, but it was an excellent way to bring the Scripture to life. You can follow Pastor Derstine's example and bring Luke 19:11-27 to life for your congregation.

You may need approval from the church treasurer to use funds for this idea. Or you may wish to use your own money and donate anything returned beyond your original investment to a specified charity. In either case, have the determined dollar amount ready to distribute at the end of your sermon.

Near the end of your sermon about Luke 19:11-27, offer a challenge to your congregation. Explain that you'd like to give them the same opportunity the master gave in Jesus' story by giving away money for the congregation to use. Tell congregation members the following guidelines:

● **Everyone who accepts the money must "invest" it in some way that potentially could result in earnings of more than the original investment.**

● **The money can be invested in any creative way that you believe will bring a return within the specified time limit.**

● **All earnings must be turned in at the time limit to be used for** (charity of your choice).

● **You can't merely return the same money at the end of the time period.**

Don't force anyone to participate, but challenge those who do want to be involved. Explain that you and your family will be participating as well. Set a specified time limit for people to turn in the results of their investments.

Suggest creative ways people can invest their funds. Offer examples such as these:

● Use the money to buy gas for your mower, then mow lawns for pay.

● Use the money to purchase craft supplies. Then sell the things you make using the supplies. (Several people who want to use this idea may want to get together and have a craft fair. The same idea could be done with baked items, with several joining for a bake sale.)

● Use the money to get advertisements printed for a sports tournament. Charge a fee per person or team entering the event.

When everyone understands the guidelines, distribute the money. Then close your sermon with a commissioning prayer, asking God to bless the efforts of the people who took the challenge.

At the end of the specified time limit, have those who participated turn in their earnings during a worship service. Have several people tell about their investment experiences and the results.

(**Note:** Some people may end up with nothing to show for their investments. Let these people know that you appreciate their efforts anyway!)

I'd like to see my pastor try some new methods other than lecture because... "We are now aware of the various learning styles of individuals. By using a variety of methods, the retention and learning potential heightens."

Complete the project by reminding people that God has given us more than money to invest. We should be investing God's gifts wisely in many areas of life—in our families, our friends, our community, and so on. Ask everyone to consider this question as they leave: **When the time comes, what return will I have to bring God on all the gifts he has given me?**

Variation: In 1994, Dr. Norm Wakefield wanted to try this idea but didn't have the large cash amount needed for everyone in his congregation. He used $16 instead. Here's how you can do what he did:

Take three envelopes and place $10 in one, $5 in another, and $1 in the third. Randomly tape the envelopes under seats. Then issue the challenge and have the people check under their seats to see if they've received the gifts. Have everyone who finds an envelope take the challenge.

Or use the $16 and simply distribute the money to the first three people who come forward to accept the challenge. Make all guidelines the same.

On Target

TOPIC: LAW VS. GRACE

SCRIPTURE: GALATIANS 3:23-29

Use this idea to demonstrate our inability to live up to God's laws and to show the greatness of God's grace.

To prepare, you'll need a box of a dozen doughnuts, an empty doughnut box, and an inflated beach ball. Determine a target that *can't* be hit with the beach ball by someone standing beside you. This might be a specific spot in the back of the balcony, a bit of paper taped to a far wall, or any other target which will be impossible to hit. (Practice this yourself a few times before your sermon to be sure!)

Place the doughnuts to the right of your pulpit or speaking area and place the empty box to your left. At the appropriate time, ask for a volunteer from the congregation. Have the volunteer stand beside you. Show the volunteer the target.

Say: **You get one chance to hit the target with this ball. If you hit the target, you get to go to "Doughnut Heaven."** Indicate the doughnut area to your right. **If you miss, you go to "Doughnut Hell."** Show people that the box to your left is empty.

Give the volunteer the ball and have him or her take only one shot, then stand in the appropriate area. Repeat the process with another volunteer.

Have as many people attempt the shot as time allows, up to 12 total. Then, with all the people still beside you, say: **With the rules I've set, no one will ever get to Doughnut Heaven. Even if you make a good shot, you still can't live up to the standard. However, I want each of you to get a taste of Doughnut Heaven with me, so I'm going to give a doughnut to each of you in spite of your inability to meet the standard.**

Distribute the doughnuts to the volunteers and let them return to their seats. Then continue your sermon, comparing this experience to our inability to live up to God's law and God giving us the free gift of grace.

Paying Attention?

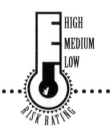

TOPIC: HEARING AND DOING GOD'S TEACHING
SCRIPTURE: JAMES 1:17-27

This idea helps people realize how quickly we forget God's instructions. For this activity each person will need a half sheet of paper and a pen or pencil.

Sometime during your sermon, say: **You've been looking at the front of our church since you sat down this morning, and if you're a regular attendee you've seen this area for weeks, months, even years. But take a minute and silently study the area at the front of the sanctuary.**

Time one minute, then say: **Now take out the sheet of paper and pencil you have. Keep your eyes on your paper and don't look up or around. I want you to draw the front of our sanctuary. Make this drawing as detailed as you can, including everything that's visible from your seat. The drawing must be done from memory. No peeking!**

Remind people that artistic ability doesn't matter, it's what was included or forgotten that's important. Give everyone a few minutes to complete his or her drawing. Then have them compare their drawings to the actual area in question. It's highly unlikely that anyone will have remembered every detail.

Check to see if people remembered things like your water glass, tapestry designs, designs on a stained-glass window, microphones, clocks and clock faces, musical instruments, and even you.

Then continue with your teaching, comparing forgetting the details of the church with the person described in James 1:23-24. If you like, have people find partners and discuss one or more of the following questions at various points during your sermon:

● **What did you leave out of your drawing? Why do you suppose you left that out?**

● **How was your forgetfulness in this activity like the person described in verses 23-24 of James 1?**

● **Why do you suppose people study God's teaching then "forget" to do what God has taught?**

● **What can you do this week to avoid "forgetting" to do God's teaching?**

Piano Movers

TOPIC: REACHING THE GOAL TOGETHER

SCRIPTURE: EPHESIANS 4:11-16

Use this object lesson to illustrate the importance of supporting one another.

At the appropriate time during your sermon, ask for a volunteer to come up front. Then ask your volunteer to move the piano (or organ, pulpit, or other large and heavy object) to a new location, such as the other side of the platform area. Your volunteer may try unsuccessfully or may simply refuse on the grounds that it's impossible to do alone. (Don't let people try so hard they hurt themselves!)

Then say: **Would anyone else like to help** (name of volunteer) **reach the goal?**

Encourage other volunteers to come up until there are enough people to accomplish the task easily. Then have them move the object. Afterward, thank your volunteers and have everyone sit down.

Continue your sermon, comparing the way people worked together to complete the goal of moving the piano to the way the church body must function together to reach the goal of being like Christ.

Popcorn Peddlers

TOPIC: TEMPTATION

SCRIPTURE: LUKE 4:1-13

Use this idea to emphasize that temptation constantly distracts our attention from God and God's Word.

A week or two before your sermon, recruit two or more volunteers to act as hawkers. They'll need popcorn, hot dogs, peanuts, or some other item to "sell" during your sermon. Go over the plan with them, arranging a cue, and instructing them to loudly announce their wares when they hear you speak the cue. Encourage hawkers to try to get at least one person to buy something. You'll also need to write the questions listed below on a transparency for an overhead projector.

Halfway into your sermon on temptation, cue your hawkers to start walking down the aisles calling out, "Popcorn! Hot dogs! Peanuts!" or whatever they are selling, as if they were in a baseball stadium. Continue your sermon, ignoring this interruption, even if some people actually buy from them.

After the hawkers have gone through the aisles and left the room, have people form groups of up to three. Place the following questions on an overhead projector for groups to refer to, then explain that trios have three to five minutes to discuss the questions.

● **What went through your mind when the hawkers came in? Explain.**

● **Were you tempted to stop listening to the sermon? Why or why not?**

● **How does temptation take your attention off God and God's Word in real life?**

● **What can we learn from this experience and from Luke 4:1-13 to help us overcome temptation?**

When the discussion is completed, allow representatives from several trios to report their group's thoughts to the congregation. Then continue with your sermon, encouraging people to avoid distracting temptations and to remain focused on God and God's Word at all times.

Trust and Obey

TOPIC: OBEDIENCE

SCRIPTURE: 1 JOHN 5:1-15

Use this idea to compare obeying another person to obeying God.

You'll need one envelope for each row (or pew) in your church. In each envelope place a note with one of the following statements written on it:

● Without speaking, command everyone in your row to do "the wave" for 30 seconds.

● Without speaking, command everyone in your row to sing the first verse of "Amazing Grace."

● Without speaking, command everyone in your row to stand and applaud for 60 seconds.

● Without speaking, command everyone in your row to read 1 John 5:1-15 aloud together.

● Without speaking, command everyone in your row to wave at the pastor until he or she waves back.

It's OK if more than one row has the same command. Place one command in each envelope and seal it. Tape these to the seat at the right end of each row.

As you begin your sermon, say: **I'd like those closest to the right end of each row to take the envelopes taped there and silently open them. Read what's inside but don't let anyone else read it.** Pause while people read. **Now do what it says.**

Allow several minutes for everyone to take part in the activity. Next, have each person find a partner from a different row and share what made following their leader's command easy or difficult. Then have partners discuss what makes it easy or difficult to follow God's commands.

Afterward, continue your sermon, explaining how 1 John 5:1-15 describes obedience to God as a way to show our love for God. Point out that we have a great tool to help us obey God's commands—the Bible.

The Wonders of Giving

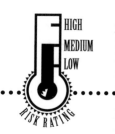

TOPIC: GIVING

SCRIPTURE: MARK 12:38-44

Just as the widow in Mark 12:38-44 gave all she had, Jesus calls us to give beyond our all to him. Use this commitment activity as a closing to your sermon to help your people follow the widow's example.

You'll need "tokens" cut from heavy paper or poster board. Each token should be about the size of a silver dollar. Distribute tokens as people enter the sanctuary, or have ushers or other assistants hand them out just before you plan to use them. Everyone will also need access to a pen or pencil.

During your sermon, after you have discussed the widow and the significance of her gift to God, have everyone take out his or her token. Say: **I'd like us to have an opportunity right now to follow the widow's example.**

Challenge people to think of what they would like to give God (such as money, time, service to others).

Say: **After you've decided what you want to give to God today, confidentially write it on your token. You don't have to include your name, just what you wish to give.**

After people have done this, allow them to come forward and place their tokens into an offering plate to symbolize their commitment to follow the widow's example and give their all to God.

I'd like to see my pastor try some new methods other than lecture because ... "Lectures are boring and dogmatic."

Worry Warts

TOPIC: WORRY AND ANXIETY
SCRIPTURE: MATTHEW 6:25-34

Although everyone will admit that worrying about a problem generally won't improve the situation, it's often difficult to stop feelings of anxiety. Use this idea to help congregation members laugh at worries and find ways of getting over the worrying habit.

During your sermon, have people form groups of up to four. Explain that this exercise will give those who consider themselves "professional worriers" a chance to prove their skills.

After you read each of the following statements, allow one minute for groups to "worry" together and determine the worst possible, most outlandish outcome of the situation. For example, the response to the first statement could be, "My husband was abducted by aliens and taken to live in a human zoo on the planet Orgblaatz."

Have representatives from a few groups report their outcomes before moving on to the next statement.

Statements to read:

● **Your spouse or teenage child or another person you dearly love is an hour late arriving home and has not called.**

● **Rumors are flying at work that someone is going to be laid off tomorrow.**

● **The phone rings at three in the morning.**

● **You've been asked to speak in front of your entire school, church, or company.**

● **A bill arrives in the mail.**

After you've gone through the groups' responses to all the statements, repeat the activity, but this time have groups determine the *best* thing that could happen. For example, in the first situation someone might say, "My daughter won the Publishers Clearing House Sweepstakes, and in the media frenzy was unable to find a phone to call and let me know." Again have a few groups share their conclusions.

Then continue your sermon, using Matthew 6:25-34 to explain how we can trust God to care for the concerns of this life. Toward the end of your sermon, have congregation members return to their

VIEW FROM THE PEW

What I like best about sermons is . . . "How they sometimes open my mind to a new understanding of God's Word."

foursomes and brainstorm ways to avoid worry and anxiety during the upcoming week. For example, congregation members might give ideas such as praying, taking immediate action to solve the problem, talking about it with friends, and so on.

Sermon Ideas for

Special
Occasions

Happy New Life!

HIGH
MEDIUM
LOW

RISK RATING

TOPIC: BECOMING A NEW CHRISTIAN (New Year's Day)
SCRIPTURE: COLOSSIANS 3:1-10

Use this idea to help congregation members gain insight from Colossians 3:1-10 and compare the changes of a new year to the changes that accompany new life in Christ.

Prepare for this activity by placing a small sheet of aluminum foil in each worship-service bulletin. The pieces of foil should be about the same size as your bulletins so they fit inside.

At the appropriate time in your sermon, have everyone remove the foil from the bulletins.

Say: **Each New Year's holiday, we look for ways to change our past, to create a new hope for the future. We turn over a new leaf, renew our resolutions, and make plans for the new things we'd like to accomplish in the coming year.**

Right now, I'd like us to examine this idea of newness that comes with a new year. Take the foil you're holding and create something entirely new from it. Reshape it into an airplane, an animal, a hat, or whatever you want.

James Cook

87

After about two minutes, have each person join one or two others to form groups of no more than three. Have each person share his or her new creation and, if necessary, explain what it is.

Then say: **Now I'd like you to somehow join your creation with those of your group members to make another entirely new object. This may require reshaping of the foil, but do what's necessary to create something new.**

Allow a minute or two for groups to do this. Have a few groups who are especially pleased with their creations share them with the entire congregation.

Then have ushers or other assistants collect the sculptures to be recycled. Explain that all of these new creations will again be reshaped as they are recycled and made into new aluminum products. Have groups discuss the following questions: **How is the way we reshaped the foil like the way we're reshaped in life? How is it different?**

Then say: **We've reshaped our used bits of foil to create new things, but God does more than simply reshape or recycle us. He makes us entirely new from the inside out.**

Continue your sermon, exploring God's creative work as it's described in Colossians 3:1-10.

Touchdown!

TOPIC: TRAINING TO WIN (Super Bowl Sunday)
SCRIPTURE: 1 CORINTHIANS 9:16-27

What listing of special occasions would be complete without Super Bowl Sunday? On that Sunday, use this idea to demonstrate the importance of training both in sports and in our Christian lives. You'll need two footballs for this idea.

Mark out two sections in the auditorium to create roughly equal teams out of the entire congregation. Designate a volunteer in each section to be a team captain. You may want to talk to the team captains before the sermon to give them a little advance warning.

Say: **In honor of the football game to be played today, we're going to have a little sports training ourselves. In a moment I'm going to give the first person in each section a football. Then**

88

we'll have a race to see which team can hand off the football, from person to person, until it reaches the last person in each section. Captains, take a minute now to get your teams ready for competition.

Have the team captains coach their sections on winning techniques. For example, they might have everyone move closer together to speed passing time, or they might have people pass imaginary footballs to see how quickly they can move.

After a few minutes of coaching, give the first person in each section a football.

Say: **Each person must receive and hand off the football until it reaches the last person in your section. That person must then stand and wave the football so I can see it. The first section to have its football finish the course wins.**

Begin the competition. Encourage sections to cheer their teammates on. When you have a winning team, have everyone else stand and cheer for the winners for 30 seconds.

Afterward, have volunteers retrieve the footballs. Then have congregation members turn to a neighbor to discuss the following questions: **What would've made our handoffs more successful? How does training give teams an edge in competition? How does training help us in our Christian life?**

Point out that the teams playing in the Super Bowl didn't get there by accident. Each player trained and competed for years to be ready when the opportunity came to play for a championship. Continue your sermon, comparing the training and reward of your handoff competition and the Super Bowl to the training and reward described by Paul in 1 Corinthians 9:16-27.

Sweet Hearts

HIGH
MEDIUM
LOW

RISK RATING

TOPIC: PERFECT LOVE (Valentine's Day)

SCRIPTURE: 1 CORINTHIANS 13:1-13

What could be more appropriate for a Valentine's Day sermon idea than the "love chapter," 1 Corinthians 13?

For this idea you'll need enough candy conversation hearts for each person to have one. Have someone sort the hearts to remove any that might be inappropriate. When you're ready to use the idea, have ushers distribute the hearts and instruct each person in the congregation to take one.

Say: **This Valentine's Day, let's take a little time to reflect on our experiences of love. First, read the phrase on your candy heart. Then find one or two people who have the same phrase on their hearts to form groups of up to three.**

Allow a minute for people with the same phrases to find each other. If a few people absolutely cannot find anyone with a match, let them join together to form pairs or trios. Then instruct all groups to read 1 Corinthians 13:1-13 together.

Say: **After you have read this passage, tell your partners about a time someone showed you the kind of love these verses describe.**

Allow several minutes for sharing. Some people may not have had any experience with the kind of love described. Don't pressure them to think of something, but later mention that only God can express this kind of love consistently.

Have several pairs or trios report the examples of love shared in their groups.

Then say: **Let's have Valentine's Day remind us not only of the love people have shown us, but also of the love God has shown us. God's love fits every description of love in this passage. God's love is perfect. And best of all, God's love never ends.**

Continue your sermon, challenging people to think during the coming week about times God has shown his perfect love to them.

HIGH
MEDIUM
LOW

RISK RATING

Spring-Cleaning

TOPIC: SPRING-CLEANING OUR HEARTS (Spring)
SCRIPTURE: MARK 7:1-23

There are people who believe the saying "Cleanliness is next to godliness" came straight from the Bible—but it didn't. However, in Mark 7:1-23 the Bible tells us that more important than clean hands or a clean home is a clean heart. Use this activity at the beginning of the spring season to demonstrate this point.

During the week before your sermon, give the church custodians a break. Leave the papers, hymnals, Bibles, and other odds and ends that are often left after a service right where they are. In fact, if your congregation isn't messy enough, stop by the sanctuary the night before you use this idea and do a bit of "cluttering" yourself.

As you begin your sermon, point out that spring is often a time of cleaning. We clean out all the winter dust and cobwebs, then open the windows to let in fresh, clean air. Then comment on the untidiness of the room and ask everyone to pitch in and help "spring-clean" the sanctuary. Have congregation members pick up bits of trash and old bulletins. Send the ushers or other assistants around with trash bags. Ask people to return song books or Bibles to their holders in the pews and put other items in their proper places as well. After cleanup is done (or after a few minutes), have people stop what they're doing and return to their seats.

Say: **Look around at how nice this room looks now. It was easy to clean our sanctuary in just a short time. But there's a more important area that needs spring-cleaning today—our hearts.**

Read Mark 7:1-23 and continue your sermon, explaining that while we can clean our outer surroundings, only Jesus can "spring-clean" our hearts.

If you like, close the sermon by singing "Create in Me a Clean Heart."

VIEW FROM THE PEW

What I like least about sermons is... "Sometimes they're long and boring."

Christ's Body

HIGH
MEDIUM
LOW

RISK RATING

TOPIC: THE LORD'S SUPPER (Maundy Thursday)

SCRIPTURE: MARK 14:12-26

In Mark 14:22 Jesus uses bread to represent his body. Other passages (such as Romans 12:1-16) speak of the church as Christ's body. Use this idea to draw together those two concepts.

You'll need several loaves of unsliced bread. At the appropriate time during your sermon, pass the bread around and instruct people to take a large chunk. (Or you may want to use dinner rolls and simply give each person one roll.) Tell congregation members not to eat their bread just yet.

Say: Just as this bread represents the body of Christ, the people of this church represent the body of Christ. Take a moment right now to look around you and quietly think of how others here act as the body of Christ.

For example, perhaps someone has invited you into his or her home and shown you hospitality. Or someone may have prepared Sunday school lessons each week to teach you or your family members. Another person may have prayed for you or offered wise advice.

Allow one or two minutes of silent reflection, then say: **Now tear off a piece of your bread and go give it to one of the people you thought of. As you give it, tell that person how he or she has demonstrated being a part of Christ's body to you. You may break as many pieces of bread and give them to as many people as you like. When someone gives you a piece of bread, go ahead and eat it. When you are done sharing bread with others, return to your seat.**

Tell visitors that you'll be acting as a stand-in in case they'd like to give bread to someone who isn't a part of the congregation. Encourage them to tear off pieces of bread to represent people they know outside the congregation and to bring those pieces to you. As they bring the bread, ask each person to share with you briefly about the people the bread represents.

Take as long as you like with this activity. If you want to draw the time to a close and people are still moving about, give a "two-minute warning" to allow people to finish.

Note: If it's appropriate within your tradition, follow this activity with a communion service. Or you may want to use this as the taking of the bread in your regular communion service.

Crucify Him!

TOPIC: JESUS' TRIAL (Good Friday)

SCRIPTURE: MARK 15:1-20

Use this creative reading of Mark 15:1-20 (NCV) to tell the story of Jesus' trial in a new and dramatic way.

Make photocopies of the "Mark 15:1-20" handout (p. 93) for
(continued on p. 96)

MARK 15:1-20

Leader: Very early in the morning, the leading priests, the older leaders, the teachers of the law, and all the Jewish council decided what to do with Jesus. They tied him, led him away, and turned him over to Pilate, the governor.

All Women: Pilate asked Jesus, "Are you the king of the Jews?"

All Men: Jesus answered, "Those are your words."

Leader: The leading priests accused Jesus of many things. So Pilate asked Jesus another question,

Everyone on the Left Side of the Church: "You can see that they are accusing you of many things. Aren't you going to answer?"

Everyone on the Right Side of the Church: But Jesus still said nothing, so Pilate was very surprised.

Leader: Every year at the time of the Passover the governor would free one prisoner whom the people chose. At that time, there was a man named Barabbas in prison who was a rebel and had committed murder during a riot. The crowd came to Pilate and began to ask him to free a prisoner as he always did.

All Women: So Pilate asked them, "Do you want me to free the king of the Jews?"

Leader: Pilate knew that the leading priests had turned Jesus in to him because they were jealous. But the leading priests had persuaded the people to ask Pilate to free Barabbas, not Jesus.

All Men: Then Pilate asked the crowd again, "So what should I do with this man you call the king of the Jews?"

Leader: They shouted, "Crucify him!"

All Women: Pilate asked, "Why? What wrong has he done?" But they shouted even louder, "Crucify him!"

All Men: Pilate wanted to please the crowd, so he freed Barabbas for them. After having Jesus beaten with whips, he handed Jesus over to the soldiers to be crucified.

Leader: The soldiers took Jesus into the governor's palace and called all the other soldiers together. They put a purple robe on Jesus and used thorny branches to make a crown for his head.

All Men: They began to call out to him, "Hail, King of the Jews!" The soldiers beat Jesus on the head many times with a stick.

All Women: They spit on him and made fun of him by bowing on their knees and worshiping him. After they finished, the soldiers took off the purple robe and put his own clothes on him again.

Leader: Then they led him out of the palace to be crucified.

MARK 15:1-20
WITH NOTES FOR ACTORS

Directions: You'll act out the scene for this reading as the rest of the congregation reads the text of the passage. Your parts add to the drama and mood of the passage and bring the event to life.

Follow the parenthetical directions and sound effects given on this script. You may wish to add costumes or props, but these are not required. One person will need to play the role of Pilate, another the role of Jesus, and another the role of Barabbas. Everyone else plays the crowd and the chief priests.

•••

(As the leader reads the first line, noisily rush into the open area in a cluster, talking among yourselves angrily. "Jesus" should be in your midst. "Pilate" should be standing silently on the opposite side of the open area.)

Leader: Very early in the morning, the leading priests, the older leaders, the teachers of the law, and all the Jewish council decided what to do with Jesus. They tied him *(pantomime this quickly)*, led him away *(begin moving your group toward Pilate)*, and turned him over to Pilate, the governor. *(Push Jesus out of your group so he stands before Pilate.)*

All Women: Pilate asked Jesus *(say these words with the congregation)*, "Are you the king of the Jews?"

All Men: Jesus answered *(say these words with the congregation)*, "Those are your words."

Leader: The leading priests accused Jesus of many things. *(Each person yell out one accusation such as "He claims to be God!" "He's breaking all our laws!" "He's no king!" "He leads people away from our laws!" and so on.)* So Pilate asked Jesus another question,

Everyone on the Left Side of the Church: *(Say these words with the congregation.)* "You can see that they are accusing you of many things. Aren't you going to answer?"

Everyone on the Right Side of the Church: But Jesus still said nothing, so Pilate was very surprised. *(Pilate shows expression of surprise.)*

Leader: Every year at the time of the Passover the governor would free one prisoner whom the people chose. *(During these lines, Barabbas runs out and stands next to Pilate. Barabbas should growl loudly and make menacing faces at Pilate and the others.)* At that time, there was a man named Barabbas in prison who was a rebel and had committed murder during a riot. The crowd came to Pilate and began to ask him to free a prisoner as he always did. *(Everyone calls out, "Free a prisoner, free a prisoner!")*

All Women: So Pilate asked them *(say these words with the congregation)*, "Do you want me to free the king of the Jews?"

Leader: Pilate knew that the leading priests had turned Jesus in to him because they were jealous. But the leading priests had persuaded the people to ask Pilate to free Barabbas, not Jesus. *(Everyone yells, "Free Barabbas! Barabbas!")*

All Men: Then Pilate asked the crowd again *(say these words with the congregation),* "So what should I do with this man you call the king of the Jews?"

Leader: They shouted, "Crucify him!" *(Begin yelling, "Crucify him!" Continue yelling until Barabbas is freed.)*

All Women: Pilate asked *(say these words with congregation),* "Why? What wrong has he done?" But they shouted even louder, "Crucify him!"

All Men: Pilate wanted to please the crowd, so he freed Barabbas for them. *(Pilate pushes Barabbas toward the others. Barabbas waves fists in victory.)* After having Jesus beaten with whips, he handed Jesus over to the soldiers to be crucified. *(Jesus hangs head as if tired and in pain. Pilate leads Jesus back to the others, who now become the soldiers. Pilate leaves the stage. Barabbas joins in with the soldiers.)*

Leader: The soldiers took Jesus into the governor's palace *(lead Jesus to center stage)* and called all the other soldiers together. They put a purple robe on Jesus and used thorny branches to make a crown for his head. *(Pantomime this.)*

All Men: They began to call out to him *(yell these words loudly several times as congregation reads),* "Hail, King of the Jews!" The soldiers beat Jesus on the head many times with a stick.

All Women: They spit on him and made fun of him by bowing on their knees and worshiping him. *(Pantomime these actions, all the time laughing loudly and cruelly.)* After they finished, the soldiers took off the purple robe and put his own clothes on him again.

Leader: *(Stop all noise and act out the rest of the reading in silence.)* Then they led him out of the palace to be crucified. *(Lead Jesus out of sight. Then have an assistant create the sound effect of loud, hard strokes of a hammer against a spike. After five or six blows of the hammer, pause for a moment of complete silence.)*

I'd like to see my pastor try some new methods other than lecture... "Just to make a good thing better."

each person in your congregation. You'll want to distribute these in your bulletin or as people enter the sanctuary.

Before your sermon, recruit up to 10 volunteers who will act out the reading as it happens. Give each volunteer a photocopy of the "Mark 15:1-20 With Notes for Actors" handout (pp. 94-95) ahead of time, and schedule a time for the volunteers to practice their parts with you doing the reading.

Make sure you have an open area where the actors can act out their parts. At the appropriate time during your sermon, lead the entire congregation in reading the text as printed on the "Mark 15:1-20" handout. It's best for the Leader to use the "Mark 15:1-20 With Notes for Actors" handout so he or she knows when to pause for action. Tell congregation members to read the lines indicated even while actors are doing their parts. The actors will add their parts to create a dramatic reading in which people can "see" the events they're reading about.

When the reading is finished, pause for a moment of complete silence, then continue your sermon as planned.

HIGH
MEDIUM
LOW

RISK RATING

Brushes With Greatness

TOPIC: LETTING GOD TOUCH OUR LIVES (Easter)

SCRIPTURE: LUKE 24:1-11

On the first Easter morning, Mary Magdalene and several other women went to Jesus' tomb. There they had an encounter that changed their lives. Use this idea to remind your people that while chance meetings with "great" people can be exciting and memorable, only meeting Jesus will truly change our lives.

As you begin your sermon, say: **Take a minute to think of a time you've had a "brush with greatness." Maybe you once shook a president's hand. Perhaps you were pumping gas when a famous athlete stopped and asked you for directions. Or you won backstage passes to meet your favorite musician.**

Give congregation members a minute to think of their "brushes with greatness," then have people share their claims to fame with the persons in front, in back, and to either side of them. If you have time, ask a few people to tell the whole congregation about the experiences they heard about.

Say: **Most people have had a brush with greatness. These encounters are fun to tell about and make for good memories, but they rarely change our lives. Now let's read about a life-changing brush with greatness someone in the Bible had.**

Read aloud Luke 24:1-11.

Say: **On that first Easter morning, the women described in this passage had a brush with true greatness—they witnessed the tomb once occupied by the risen Christ. The results of that encounter forever changed their lives—and the lives of millions since.**

Continue with your sermon, focusing on the change that occurs in our lives when our brush with greatness is meeting Jesus.

Hugs and Kisses

TOPIC: HONORING PARENTS (Mother's Day or Father's Day)

SCRIPTURE: EPHESIANS 6:1-4

Ephesians 6:1-4 reminds us that God has commanded us to honor our parents. Use this affirmation idea on Mother's and/or Father's Day to give people the opportunity to honor parents.

You'll need several baskets or bowls filled with Hershey's Hugs and Hershey's Kisses. Place these in locations where people have easy access to them, such as at the end of every third or fourth pew, or at the front and back of the sanctuary.

When you're ready to honor the parents, read Ephesians 6:1-4 aloud, then say: **This passage reminds us of one of the Ten Commandments—Honor your parents. Let's take time now to obey God's command and honor our mothers (or fathers) by giving them Hugs and Kisses of affirmation.**

Point out to congregation members where the candy Hugs and Kisses are. Have each person take several pieces of candy to share with mothers (or fathers) around them. Encourage people to give Hugs and Kisses to their own parents, parents whom they respect, parents of friends, and even people who have been "spiritual parents" to them. Have ushers help out to make sure every mother (or father) receives at least one candy.

Have congregation members share an affirming word with the recipient as they give each Hug and Kiss. For example, people might

One encouraging thought I'd like to share with people who deliver sermons is... "Always rely on the Holy Spirit for direction in writing or delivering your sermons."

say, "Though I don't say it often enough, I really do love you!" or "Thanks for caring enough to help me grow in my relationship with God."

Afterward, say: **These candy Hugs and Kisses are a token expression of the love and respect we have for our mothers (or fathers). Let's remember this command to honor our parents and show them the same love and respect each day.**

Continue your sermon.

HIGH
MEDIUM
LOW

RISK RATING

Take Five

TOPIC: GOD'S REST (Summer)

SCRIPTURE: HEBREWS 4:1-13

VIEW FROM THE PEW

I'd like to see my pastor try some new methods other than lecture because...
"Different styles...of communication make the message fresh and exciting. This makes people anticipate what the sermon will be like next week."

Use this idea on a relaxing summer day as you talk about God's rest described in Hebrews 4:1-13.

Before reading the Scripture text for your sermon, tell everyone to get as comfortable as they possibly can.

Encourage people to recline, lean on the shoulders of others near them, put up their feet, loosen their ties, take off their shoes, even stretch out in the aisle if they like! When people are fully relaxed, ask them to close their eyes as you read aloud about God's promised rest in Hebrews 4:1-13.

After reading, have everyone find a partner and discuss these questions. (Allow one minute after you read each question for partners to discuss it.)

● **How did you make yourself comfortable here in the sanctuary?**

● **What feelings did you have as you heard about God's promised rest while you were relaxing here?**

● **What's most appealing for you about the prospect of entering God's rest?**

Say: **Summer is a time of rest. Kids off school. Relaxing in a hammock with a glass of lemonade. Lazy days at the beach. A much needed vacation. But even deeper than our need for summer rest is our need for God's rest.**

Then continue with your sermon, explaining that although we can't be exactly sure what God's rest will be like, we *can* be sure that God will keep his promise of rest for those who place their faith in Jesus.

Free at Last

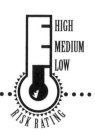

TOPIC: FREEDOM (Independence Day)

SCRIPTURE: GALATIANS 4:4-7

The topic of freedom is always appropriate near Independence Day. Use this idea to move beyond the discussion of our country's freedom to the freedom Christians have through Jesus.

You'll need several rolls of dark-colored crepe paper. You'll need enough to make several streamers that can go down each side of each row, so people in the pews will be blocked from getting out. Leave the streamers at the back of the church, ready for use.

Before your sermon, recruit ushers or other assistants to help you with this idea. Explain to them that when you give the signal (such as a nod of the head), they're to unwind the streamers and attach three or four rows of streamers along the sides of the pews or seats, creating a streamer "fence" that leaves everyone "trapped" in their seats.

On the appointed day, early in your sermon, secretly cue your assistants. Continue making your opening comments as this activity is going on, ignoring the actions or reaction of the people in the congregation. When everyone is safely "fenced" in, say: **Turn to someone near you and describe the thoughts going through your head right now.**

What makes a sermon memorable for me is . . . "Bringing it to life."

PASTOR WAGMAN KNEW HE WAS ON A ROLL WHEN THE CONGREGATION STARTED DOING THE WAVE.

If time allows, invite several volunteers to share their thoughts with the congregation as a whole. Then continue your sermon on Galatians 4:4-7, comparing being trapped in sin to being trapped in the pew. Leave the streamers up for the entire sermon.

End your message by declaring the freedom Christ bought with his death and resurrection. As a symbol that we can share in that freedom, have ushers "free" everyone by removing the streamers to dismiss the congregation.

Get Off My Pew!

TOPIC: CHANGE (Autumn)

SCRIPTURE: HEBREWS 11:1-16

Use this idea when summer begins changing to autumn to help congregation members learn how God can use change to strengthen the faith of his people.

Before your sermon, photocopy the "'Get Off My Pew!' Discussion Questions" on page 101 and tape a copy under both ends of each pew or row.

During your sermon, say: **We are now in a season of change. Summer is giving way to fall. Autumn leaves are turning brown and falling to the ground. The weather is getting colder; summer vacations are over. And now it's time for another change here in our sanctuary.**

Have everyone stand and collect his or her belongings. Then say: **Please move to the pew to your right. Those on the far right side of the room, please cross over and sit in a pew on the far left.**

After everyone has changed places, instruct the members of the congregation to form groups of five to eight (while remaining in their rows). Have each group remove the discussion questions from under the end of the pew and share responses to the questions with one another.

After discussion time, ask the questions again from the pulpit, one at a time, and allow several groups to share the results of their discussions.

Then say: **A change of seasons, a change of seats, and changes in life are sometimes difficult to face, but as Hebrews**

(continued on p. 102)

······························

"GET OFF MY PEW!"
DISCUSSION QUESTIONS

● What feelings did you have when you were asked to change seats? Explain.

● What goes on inside you when you face changes in real life? Explain.

● When was a time that a change in your life strengthened your faith in God?

Permission to photocopy this handout granted for local church use. Copyright © 1995 Mike and Amy Nappa. Published in *Bore No More! 70 Creative Ways to Involve Your Audience in Unforgettable Bible Teaching* by Group Publishing, Inc., Box 481, Loveland, CO 80539.

"GET OFF MY PEW!"
DISCUSSION QUESTIONS

● What feelings did you have when you were asked to change seats? Explain.

● What goes on inside you when you face changes in real life? Explain.

● When was a time that a change in your life strengthened your faith in God?

Permission to photocopy this handout granted for local church use. Copyright © 1995 Mike and Amy Nappa. Published in *Bore No More! 70 Creative Ways to Involve Your Audience in Unforgettable Bible Teaching* by Group Publishing, Inc., Box 481, Loveland, CO 80539.

11:1-16 illustrates, God often uses change to strengthen the faith of those who follow him.

Continue with your sermon on this passage and the topic of change.

Record-Breaking Thanks

TOPIC: THANKFULNESS (Thanksgiving)

SCRIPTURE: LUKE 17:11-19

Use this idea to help people give thanks to God in a big way!

You'll need a length of shelf paper or butcher paper to run the length of one entire wall of your sanctuary. (If you can't find one sheet long enough, tape several sheets together.) Attach the paper to the selected wall where it can be easily reached. If you have children in your worship service, be sure they'll be able to reach the paper as well. You'll also need pens or markers available for everyone. Make sure the ink won't bleed through the paper onto the wall.

During your sermon on Luke 17:11-19, say: **We're often no better than the nine who went merrily on their way. We pray and pray for God to answer our requests, yet when God responds, we smile and go on our way just as these men did.**

Today let's take time to thank God for as many things as we can. In fact, let's see if we can list so many things we're thankful for that our list sets a world record!

Direct everyone's attention to the blank paper on the wall. Say: **Let's make this the biggest thank you letter ever to God by listing on this paper everything we can thank God for.**

Ask people to get up, go over to the wall, and begin writing their thanks to God. Remind people that we can be thankful for other people, things, events, good times, bad times, Jesus, our hope, our church, our leaders, our country, nature, and much more. If there isn't enough room for everyone to write all at once, have groups of people take turns at the wall. Lead others in a time of singing songs of praise to God until it's their turn at the wall. When everyone has had a turn, complete your sermon.

Leave the letter of thanks up for several weeks, allowing people to add to it. Then, if you like, take a picture of it and send the picture along with the measurements of the paper and the number of items listed to *The Guinness Book of Records.* Who knows? Your church might have set the record for the longest thank you letter!

The address for *The Guinness Book of Records* is: 33 London Rd., Enfield, Middlesex, England EN2 6DJ.

Dressed for Winter

TOPIC: THE ARMOR OF GOD (Winter)

SCRIPTURE: EPHESIANS 6:10-20

Protective winter clothing is the closest thing to armor most people today wear. Use this activity on a cold winter day to illustrate the armor of God.

As you begin your sermon, have congregation members stand and put on their coats, gloves, sweaters, and so on, just as if they were preparing to go back out into the cold weather. When everyone is dressed, say: **Look around at what others are wearing.** Pause while people look. **This is how we dress to battle the elements of winter—covering as much of our bodies as possible to protect ourselves from the cold.**

Allow people to remove their coats and other outerwear and be seated again.

Say: **Just as we wear specific kinds of clothing to protect us in our battle against the cold of winter, God has provided spiritual armor to protect us in our battle against evil.**

Continue your sermon. As you speak about the various parts of God's armor, compare them to various items worn or used during nasty weather. For example, an umbrella might be compared to the shield of faith, and snow boots might represent feet wearing the Good News of peace.

Variation: If it would be too difficult for the entire congregation to put on their coats, choose three or four volunteers and send them out during the sermon to get their coats and model them for the congregation.

HIGH
MEDIUM
LOW

RISK RATING

Let the Celebration Begin!

TOPIC: CELEBRATE JESUS (Advent)

SCRIPTURE: LUKE 2:8-20

VIEW FROM THE PEW

One encouraging thought I'd like to share with people who deliver sermons is . . . "A sermon that pierces the heart of the people can explode them to action. Sermons can be a powerful tool for the Lord."

Use this celebration idea to help congregation members catch the joy displayed by the angels and shepherds who were present at Christ's birth.

During your sermon, say: **Let's follow the example of the angels and shepherds whose celebration of Christ's birth is described in Luke 2:8-20. Let's kick off the Advent season with our own celebration of Christ's birth right now!**

Lead your congregation in the First Christmas Party of the Year by using as many of these celebration ideas as you like:

● Begin with the lighting of the first Advent candle. Have the family in your church who has most recently had a baby light the candle as Luke 2:8-20 is read aloud.

● Have a time of singing favorite Christmas hymns and carols. Allow people to request their favorite songs and sing one verse of these songs together.

● Have ushers (or others who have volunteered ahead of time) serve warm spiced apple cider. Or have a table with refreshments and beverages where people can serve themselves.

● Ask each family or individual to join with another family. Then have each person tell a favorite Christmas memory or a favorite Christmas tradition his or her family shares.

Finish your time with a short message about why Jesus' birth gives us a reason to celebrate all year long.

No Random Gift

HIGH
MEDIUM
LOW

RISK RATING

TOPIC: JESUS IS A GIFT FROM GOD (Christmas)
SCRIPTURE: MATTHEW 1:18-25

The birth of Christ is commonly celebrated by giving gifts to those we love. Use this idea to remind congregation members that Jesus was the first and best Christmas gift ever.

You'll need a small present that would be enjoyed by any member of your congregation (such as a gift certificate to a local restaurant or department store). Wrap the present in bright Christmas paper. You will also need to write directions such as the ones that follow on separate slips of paper. Use these directions as a guide, creating and including as many more as you like.

Directions:
- Move the gift three people to the right.
- Move the gift 10 people back.
- Move the gift three people forward and then one person toward the nearest clock.
- Move the gift four people in the direction of the piano.
- Move the gift eight people forward, then three people back.
- Move the gift to the closest person wearing red earrings.
- Move the gift to the closest person wearing a green tie (or shirt).
- Move the gift randomly so 15 different people touch it once.

Fold the slips of paper with directions on them and place them in a bowl or other container.

During your sermon, hand the gift to anyone in the congregation and explain that it can't be opened yet. Then draw one of the slips of paper (or have a volunteer from the congregation draw it) and read the directions.

Move the gift as directed, then repeat the drawing of a new slip of paper. Continue as time allows or until you run out of directions. Have the last person to hold the gift open it and tell everyone what he or she has received. Let this person know that he or she may keep the gift.

Then say: **It's fun to randomly give and receive a gift like that. But this Christmas, let's remember that the gift of Jesus' birth wasn't just a random gift for some lucky person who happened to be sitting in the right seat. The gift of God's Son that**

VIEW FROM THE PEW

I'd like to see my pastor try some new methods other than lecture because...
"Things that move you and make a strong impression stay with you SO much longer."

first Christmas was given to you, me, and the whole world. And that gift is truly the greatest gift ever given.

Continue your sermon, encouraging people to receive the greatest gift ever this Christmas season.

I've Got an Announcement!

TOPIC: NEW BIRTH (Birthdays or Birth of a Child)

SCRIPTURE: JOHN 3:1-21

Use this activity to help people think about the spiritual rebirth Christians experience. This idea could be used at any time, but we suggest using it on a week when you'll be having baby dedications, or on the week of *your* birthday, whether physical or spiritual.

You'll need sheets of paper, pens, and markers or crayons. Place several sheets of paper, along with a container of writing instruments, at the end of each pew or row.

As you discuss John 3:1-21, say: **It's likely that when you were born, your parents sent cards to friends and relatives announcing your birth. But it's unlikely that anyone here had a birth announcement sent out telling of your spiritual rebirth into God's family. When we experience that spiritual rebirth described in John 3:1-21, it's worth announcing. So let's take time now to make spiritual birth announcements. Create an announcement about your rebirth into God's family or about another important event in your life.** By giving congregation members this second option, you won't single out non-Christians and they'll be free to participate without pressure.

Have those sitting on the ends of the aisles distribute the paper to those on their row. (Markers and other writing instruments may need to be shared.) Have congregation members create cards or letters telling about when they became Christians (or experienced other significant events). Ask people to include any information they know, such as the date or age the person became a Christian, circumstances leading up to the decision, people involved, and so on.

Encourage people to be creative, but remind everyone that artistic ability isn't required (stick figures will do, if needed). Birth announcements could be worded like movie posters ("Now Appearing in God's Family—Me!"), like book reviews ("The Start of a Real Page-Turner, With a Happily-Ever-After Ending), or whatever else congregation members might think of.

Allow five to 10 minutes for people to work on their announcements. Then have congregation members form groups of up to four members and share their announcements with one another (if they want to).

Continue your sermon, pointing out how the joy that comes with a new birth can be multiplied through eternity when a person experiences rebirth in Jesus. Encourage people to take their announcements home and keep them as reminders of the joy of new birth, whether physical or spiritual!

Wedded Bliss

TOPIC: MARRIAGE (Weddings)
SCRIPTURE: EPHESIANS 5:21-33

Use this idea during a wedding to allow audience members to expand on Paul's advice for marriage in Ephesians 5:21-33. Be sure to describe the activity to the bride and groom and obtain their approval before including it in a wedding ceremony.

For this activity you'll need enough heart-shaped papers for all wedding guests. You may wish to cut these hearts yourself or purchase them at a stationery or specialty-paper store. (You'll probably impress the bride and groom if you select paper to match the wedding colors!)

As you are addressing the couple to be married and their guests, say: **In Ephesians 5:21-33, Paul gave great advice for building a strong, lasting, and Christ-honoring marriage. Put your spouse first. Love each other. Respect each other.**

Address the audience and say: **Think about what advice you might give to this couple to help them put into practice Paul's words to love and respect each other, and thus build a strong, lasting, and Christ-honoring marriage.**

After a moment of "think time," have ushers distribute the paper hearts and pens. Say: **Write your words of advice to** (names of bride and groom) **on your heart-shaped paper.**

Tell wedding guests that their advice will be bound into a booklet to be given to the bride and groom and kept as a practical reminder of Paul's advice. Then allow a moment for people to write their advice.

When everyone is finished, explain that someone will be waiting at the exit to collect these as everyone leaves. (Be sure you have one or two people ready to do this.) Then continue with the ceremony.

Afterward, take the heart-shaped papers and make them into a booklet for the bride and groom. This can be done by having a hole drilled in the stack of hearts at a print shop and tying a ribbon through the stack. Deliver the gift to the newlyweds when they return from their honeymoon.

First on My Agenda

TOPIC: BEING READY FOR CHRIST'S RETURN
(Ascension Day)

SCRIPTURE: 1 THESSALONIANS 5:1-11

Use this idea to help your congregation look forward to the greatest special occasion yet to come—Christ's return.

You'll need a 3x5 card and a pen for each person.

At the appropriate time during your sermon, say: **Perhaps you're the kind of person who says, "Someday I'm going to do that."** For example, you might say, "Someday I'm going to learn to sky-dive," "Someday I'm going to visit Disney World," or "Someday I'll write a book." Well, "someday" will never come unless you start planning for it.

Have ushers distribute the 3x5 cards and pens. Say: **Make a list of at least five things you want to do before Christ returns.**

Allow several minutes for people to compile their lists. Then have several people call out items from their lists. Form groups of no more than five by having people turn to their neighbors. Then read aloud 1 Thessalonians 5:1-11 aloud. Have groups discuss the following questions: **What does this passage tell us about preparing for the future? What should top our list of things to do before Christ returns? How can our plans today help us reach our goals tomorrow?**

What I like best about sermons is . . . "To learn something."

After volunteers share their responses, continue your sermon, explaining why being ready for Christ's return is so important. You might want to use this sermon to explain how to become a Christian as the first step in preparing for Jesus' return.

I THINK OUR CONGREGATION HAS BEEN WATCHING TOO MUCH SPORTS ON T.V.

Epilogue

Child: "Church? Church is boring! Didn't <u>you</u> think church was boring when you were a kid?"

Parent: "Well, sure, I hated going...You may end up hating church, too, but you have to come by that feeling honestly. You have to put in the pew time, like Mom and I did."

Child: "Oh. (Pause) What if I like it?"

—From a Doonesbury cartoon by Garry Trudeau

Now What?

Well, you've reached the end of this book, but does that mean bore-no-more ideas must be over for you and your congregation? Absolutely not!

With a little thought, prayer, and preparation, you can create your own sermon memory-makers. Just follow these eight easy steps:

Step 1: Pray. Creativity begins with God. (Would *you* have thought of creating a giraffe?) So before you do anything else, take time to ask the Creator of all to help you think of a meaningful, interactive experience to illustrate your sermon.

Step 2: Select your Scripture passage and topic. Use whatever method you normally do for selecting these.

Step 3: Inventory your resources. List things you can use quickly and easily in a sermon setting. First, think about things that will already be in the building (such as pews, hymnals, Bibles, people, purses, ties, jewelry, lights, microphones, musical instruments, keys, pens, and so on). Next, think of thinks that can easily be carried into the worship service (such as 3x5 cards, bulletin handouts, a ball or two, small pieces of candy, envelopes, masking tape, butcher paper, newsprint, markers, and so on).

Step 4: Identify exactly which point you want to illustrate with your interactive idea. Look over the outline of your sermon. Which point would best lend itself to an interactive experience? Which point do you most want people to remember?

Step 5: Brainstorm three or four interactive experiences for which you can answer "Yes" to the following questions:

● Does the experience clearly and easily tie into the point it's to illustrate?

● Does the experience get at people's "feeling level," bringing a connection to real life and making the illustration meaningful?

● With the exception of a dramatic skit, does the experience involve everyone in the congregation in *doing* something, no matter how many people might be attending the worship service?

● Does the experience challenge people to think? Does it go beyond rote memorization and encourage people to mull over what they're learning?

● Does the experience provide an opportunity for people to interact with others (through discussion, problem solving, and so on)?

● Is the experience practical and doable? Can it be easily and appropriately carried out in a sermon setting?

Step 6: Choose one or two ideas from your brainstormed list. Identify exactly how you want the idea to tie in with your sermon, then choose the experience that's most likely going to work best. (You may want to choose more than one idea.)

Step 7: Collect supplies (if any) and practice explaining or facilitating the activity. Talk through the illustration with someone else—a spouse, another pastor, or someone from the congregation. Anticipate any potential technical difficulties or negative responses and prepare for them. Make sure your directions are clear and easy to understand and follow.

Step 8: Rely on the Holy Spirit to change lives! Remember, the best illustration in the world is useless if the Holy Spirit's heart-changing power is absent. Your job is to be the instrument through which learning can occur. The Holy Spirit's job is to use your efforts to bring that learning to life in the heart of the listener. Simply do your job and trust that the Holy Spirit will help.

And so the adventure that began when you first opened this book continues. God bless you as you continue making a difference in the lives of the people who hear your words!

RISK-RATING INDEX

"Low Risk" Illustrations

"Medium Risk" Illustrations

"Medium Risk" Illustrations

"High Risk" Illustrations

SCRIPTURE INDEX

Evaluation of Bore No More! 70 Creative Ways to Involve Your Audience in Unforgettable Bible Teaching

Please help Group Publishing, Inc. continue providing innovative and useable resources for pastors, teachers and speakers by taking a moment to fill out and send us this evaluation. Thanks!

• • •

1. As a whole, this book has been (circle one):

Not much help   Very Helpful

1   2   3   4   5   6   7   8   9   10

2. The things I liked best about this book were:

3. This book could be improved by:

4. One thing I'll do differently because of this book is:

5. Optional Information:

Name _____

Street Address_____

City _____ State _____Zip _____

Phone Number _____ Date _____

Do You Have a Great Idea for a Way to Involve Your Audience in Bible Teaching?

If so, we'd love to see it! Simply write your idea in the space below (or on a separate sheet of paper), then send it to:

Bore No More Ideas
Group Publishing, Inc.
Box 481
Loveland, CO 80539

If we decide to publish your idea in a future book, we'll pay you $30 and list your name as a contributor to the book. (We'll also give you a free copy of the book so you can see all the creative ideas other people sent us!) Be sure to include your name, address, and phone number with your idea.

• • •

Name _____

Street Address _____

City _____ State _____ Zip _____

Phone Number _____ Date _____

THE IDEA

_____

_____

_____

_____

_____

_____

_____

_____

_____

_____

ANCIENT SECRETS of the BIBLE
COLLECTORS SERIES

PERFECT FOR CHURCH, CLASSROOM, AND HOME USE.

You'll see biblically accurate dramatizations. Expert testimony. Faith-building experiments. Thought-provoking debate. And you'll get a FREE 16-page Discussion Guide with each video. Perfect for Sunday school classes, home Bible studies, mid-week and youth group meetings, home schooling, adult courses, or whenever you want to explore Scripture.

WHICH OF THESE 13 VIDEOS WOULD YOU MOST LIKE TO ADD TO YOUR PERSONAL OR CHURCH COLLECTION?

Ark of the Covenant: Lost or Hidden Away?	ISBN 1-55945-733-3
Battle of David and Goliath: Truth or Myth?	ISBN 1-55945-729-5
The Fiery Furnace: Could Anyone Survive It?	ISBN 1-55945-736-8
Moses' Red Sea Miracle: Did It Happen?	ISBN 1-55945-731-7
Moses' Ten Commandments: Tablets From God?	ISBN 1-55945-732-5
Noah's Ark: Fact or Fable?	ISBN 1-55945-725-2
Noah's Ark: Was There a Worldwide Flood?	ISBN 1-55945-726-0
Noah's Ark: What Happened To It?	ISBN 1-55945-727-9
Samson: Strongman Hero or Legend?	ISBN 1-55945-735-X
Shroud of Turin: Fraud or Evidence of Christ's Resurrection?	ISBN 1-55945-737-6
Sodom and Gomorrah: Legend or Real Event?	ISBN 1-55945-730-9
Tower of Babel: Fact or Fiction?	ISBN 1-55945-728-7
Walls of Jericho: Did They Tumble Down?	ISBN 1-55945-734-1

GET IN ON THE SECRETS! EACH VIDEO IS GUARANTEED TO START DISCUSSIONS, TEACH BIBLICAL TRUTHS, AND SHED LIGHT ON BIBLE MYSTERIES! GET YOUR COPY TODAY!

From Group, the Innovator in Christian Education!

Why Nobody Learns Much Of Anything At Church: And How To Fix It

Thom & Joani Schultz

Here's a hard-hitting, provocative evaluation of learning in the church...and practical solutions for improving how your church educates.

Anyone who teaches children, youth, or adults about the Christian faith will:
- see revealing evidence why people aren't learning at church;
- discover why Sunday school attendance is plummeting;
- learn how a generation has been trained not to think;
- grasp why people listen to sermons week after week but can't remember what they heard; and
- explore how your curriculum materials may be teaching the opposite of what you intend.

And you'll find loads of practical help—step-by-step plans to help you launch a new revolution of learning in your church. You'll discover...
- how to adjust your emphasis from teaching to learning (there's a BIG difference);
- how to teach LESS so your people learn MORE;
- an approach to learning that Jesus perfected—totally involving people through active experiences;
- how to create learning environments that result in changed lives;
- how more student talk (and less teacher talk) will lead to deeper understanding, greater life application of biblical truths, and growing attendance in church classes; and
- innovative solutions that will double your people's retention of the messages in your lessons, sermons, Bible studies, programs, and classes.

This well-researched book reveals how we are all victims of an old approach to teaching and learning and how we've been programmed to repeat the mistakes of the past. But there's hope! Through a fascinating tour of Christian and secular emerging educational models, Thom and Joani Schultz show you how your church can reinvent its approaches to learning.

Hardcover	ISBN 1-55945-155-6
Paperback	ISBN 1-55945-907-7
Video	ISBN 1-55945-195-5

Order today from your local Christian bookstore, or write:
Group Publishing, Box 485, Loveland, CO 80539.

INNOVATIVE RESOURCES
FOR YOUR YOUTH MINISTRY

The Youth Worker's Encyclopedia of Bible-Teaching Ideas

Explore the two most comprehensive idea-books available for youth workers! Discover more than 350 creative ideas in each of these 400-page encyclopedias—there's at least one idea for each and every book of the Bible. Find ideas for...retreats and overnighters, adventures, special projects, parties, devotions, skits, and much more! Plus, you can use these ideas for groups of all sizes in any setting. Discover exciting new ways to teach each book of the Bible to your youth group.

Old Testament: ISBN 1-55945-184-X
New Testament: ISBN 1-55945-183-1

Group's Tube-a-loon™ Book

Jam-packed with 50 totally tubular games featuring the Group Tube-a-loon™, this is the wackiest game book ever! And just what is a Tube-a-loon? It's a 7-foot-long air-filled tube that's tons of outrageous fun. You and your kids can throw a long bomb, joust with a black knight, bat a ball, squirm like a worm, and more. Use these activities, team-builders, and Bible applications with groups of all sizes, kids of all ages, in all kinds of places. Comes with 5 Tube-a-loons in a variety of colors.

ISBN 1-55945-798-8

Hot Talk-Starter Videos

Get your teenagers really talking with this exciting video series. Each video presents four hot topics that are guaranteed to start discussions and get kids exploring biblical answers to controversy. Plus, each video comes with a complete leaders guide.

Series 1: Teen Suicide, An Atheist's Beliefs, Dating: He Says/She Says, Teenagers in the KKK — ISBN 1-55945-259-5

Series 2: Pregnant Teenager, R-Rated Movies, What's a Monk?, Hooked on Gambling — ISBN 1-55945-274-9

Series 3: The Rapture of 1992, Underage Smoker, A Visit to a New Age Store, The Gang Life — ISBN 1-55945-275-7

Series 4: Gay Rights, Palm Reading, Body Image: Glamour Shots, Homeless Teenagers — ISBN 1-55945-276-5

Order today from your local Christian bookstore, or write:
Group Publishing, Box 485, Loveland, CO 80539.